Love and Sex in Marriage:

A Medical Doctor's Guide to the Sensual Union

John Deaton, M.D.

Parker Publishing Company, Inc.
West Nyack, New York

.

Library of Congress Cataloging in Publication Data

Deaton, John G
    Love and sex in marriage.

    Bibliography: p.
    Includes index.
    1. Sex in marriage. 2. Sex instruction. I. Title.
HQ31.D38   301.41'8   78-3644
ISBN 0-13-540856-3

Printed in the United States of America

To Mimi

Other books by John Deaton, M.D.

Markets for the Medical Author
New Parts for Old, The Age of Organ Transplants
A Medical Doctor's Guide to Youth, Health and Longevity
Below the Belt, A Book about the Pelvic Organs

*How this book can
improve your marriage . . .*

This book was written to show how you and your mate can enjoy the richest, happiest sex life that is possible. It is a mature book, and it was written for the married person. You may be aware of other books on sex—books that treat this important subject in a distasteful or sensational manner. You won't find that here. I have given this subject the dignity it deserves—without sacrificing clarity in the step-by-step instructions.

New Research Made This Book Possible

It is only now that an authoritative marriage manual such as this one could be written. Scientific research is the reason. First Dr. Alfred C. Kinsey, then Drs. William Masters and Virginia Johnson, and in recent years many others have given us much-needed information about the causes of sexual difficulties and how to correct them. This new knowledge has meant better sex for thousands and thousands of people, and it can mean the same for you. In writing "Love and Sex in Marriage," I've drawn from scores of scientific articles, books and monographs, as well as my own professional experience. My purpose has been to give you the most up-to-date information in the best possible way. The book is especially meant for the couple who have no sexual problems, but just want to get more pleasure out of marriage.

How You, Too, Can Enjoy a Sensual Union

At its best, sex is more than a reproductive act. It is a gift from one marriage partner to another, a way of loving and self-expression and renewal. It's also fun. In fact, nothing else in life can bring so complete a happiness as sexual fulfillment. The husband and wife who truly enjoy sex have what I choose to call a Sensual Union. They've learned about each other's needs and desires, and have discovered the pleasure of saying "yes." They stay out of ruts by trying new things. They find excitement in each other, and they show their love. Most of all, they enjoy sex. This book was written to show how any couple can have a Sensual Union.

The first four chapters take up the subjects of love and sex in marriage, sexual intercourse, and the role of a man and of a woman in sexual love. Then, Chapters 5 and 6 contain the two-week program to show how you and your mate can begin to get more pleasure out of a Sensual Union. Other chapters deal with problem areas in the sexual relationship, sex during and after pregnancy, and the ways to enjoy sex despite having a chronic illness. One chapter tells how a woman can improve her sexual performance, and another shows how a man can do the same. Chapter 10 takes up the very important subject of sexual happiness during middle age and later years. The last two chapters are devoted to birth control methods for a woman and for a man, respectively. You'll find the information you need to choose the birth control method that is right for you.

The One and Only Way to Improve Your Marriage

Throughout this book I have used numerous examples of actual couples with sexual difficulties. By watching them work through their problems, you may be able to solve similar difficulties or check them before they get started. I respect the right of all persons to privacy. For this reason I have changed names, joggled times and identities, and in some instances drawn a composite patient in the enclosed case histories. One thing is certain. The one and only way to improve your marriage is by doing it together.

Both of you should read this book. By the time you've finished the first six chapters, you'll know new and exciting ways of enjoying marital intimacies. You'll also be talking about your feelings in a more refreshing and open way than ever before. That alone can be fun—and therapeutic.

Not the least of what you'll learn is how the body responds to sexual stimulation, the what and why of sexual function. Sex education? Absolutely! For too long this has been a neglected subject in this country. In fact, sexual ignorance seems to be an Anglo-Saxon tradition. Years ago it was thought that a naive young woman brought zest to the marriage bed. To her new husband was left the job of teaching her about sex, and the complete course and final examination were held on the wedding night. Given a choice, most women would prefer to have some idea of what to expect ahead of time. And so would most men! Marriage, after all, is a mutual commitment of two people for life. Sex is an enjoyable part of that commitment. It's too important a subject to leave to chance.

John Deaton, M.D.

Table of Contents

9

13. *Birth Control Methods for the Wife (Cont.)*

14. *Birth Control Methods for the Husband*

1

How to Attain Sexual Happiness in Marriage

Most couples remember the months right after marriage as being among the happiest of their lives. They were able to share their love openly and intimately, and doing so brought them great pleasure. Happy couples quickly learn an important fact. They discover that *marriage is both an ending and a beginning*. It is the end of the courtship, and it is the beginning of a lifetime partnership in giving. Sexual relations are a part of this giving, and mutually satisfying sexual intercourse contributes to a happy marriage. You can do four things to have sexual happiness in marriage. They are:

Four Ways to Attain Sexual Happiness in Marriage

#1. Love Your Husband or Wife.
#2. Learn Your Mate's Sexual Needs and Respond to Them.
#3. Learn to Receive Pleasure by Giving It.
#4. Be Aware that Sexual Love Can Take Many Forms.

The Most Fulfilling Thing in Life

Few who have had it will doubt that sexual happiness in marriage is the most fulfilling thing in life. Intercourse gives pleasure to both marital partners, but it is more than something that feels good. It is a physical and emotional union, a bond of love. The best thing about it is that it can get better with the passage of time. This happens when the husband and wife love one another and respond to each other's needs. Let's begin by looking at how love fits into the recipe for sexual happiness.

#1. Love Your Husband or Wife.

What is love? Who can say? It's the special warmth you feel for someone; an inner glow that comes from sharing life with another person. It's the happiness you and your mate feel, your certain knowledge that the two of you are right for each other. You may have fallen for a smile, a dimple, a wisp of curly hair or a pair of soft brown eyes; more likely, you just fell, and weren't sure why. Physical attraction is part of love, and forms the basis of a sexual relationship. However, love goes far beyond the physical. It is a total commitment of mind and body. The two are tied together more closely than you may have realized.

Marabel Morgan, author of the book *The Total Woman*, wrote that a woman's brain is her most important sex organ. "Unless it says, 'Okay, go ahead,' she can't get sexual fulfillment. In other words, she has to want to be turned on before she can be."[1] Love is behind a wife's desire for sex with her husband, and the same is true of a man's desire for his wife. Dr. David Reuben, author of *Any Woman Can!*, had this to say about what love means to a man: "Exotic sexual techniques are not nearly as important to a man as the knowledge that his wife loves him, cares about him and wants

---

[1]Marabel Morgan, *The Total Woman*, Fleming H. Revell, Old Tappan, New Jersey, 1973.

him sexually. . . . The foundation for sexual happiness—or misery—is laid not in the bedroom, but at the breakfast table.''[2]

Love can work its wonders in many ways. A few years ago I heard about a woman who used love to overcome her husband's indifference. She was

The Wife Who Started Cooking and Couldn't Stop

Barbara W. and her husband got married shortly before he left for Vietnam. Except for an all-too-brief R & R, she didn't see him for a year. And when he did come home, he'd changed. Barbara had waited for him and wanted his undivided affection, but she didn't get it. Wayne, the husband, began phoning his old Army buddies, and going out in the evenings to see them. Barbara felt that her marriage was slipping away. She confided her feelings to a friend, and asked for advice.

"Barbara," the woman said, "just love him! Show him he's the one man in the world for you. Do something marvelous for him! Shower him with love."

On the way home, Barbara remembered something she could do for Wayne. He dearly loved her chocolate chip cookies, yet she hadn't made them a single time since he'd been home. Why—she suddenly remembered—she'd meant to have the house full of them when Wayne got back! She hadn't. She'd been too excited about meeting him at the airport to do any cooking. Well, now she had her chance. She bought the ingredients and began cooking. Her husband was gone for the afternoon, but when he returned that evening he broke into a smile of delight. Waiting for him just inside the front door was a plate of fresh chocolate chip cookies. There were cookies on the sofa, cookies on the rug, cookies on the coffee table. The kitchen cabinets were covered with chocolate chip cookies.

---

[2]D. Reuben, *Any Woman Can!*, David McKay, New York, 1971.

Barbara looked up from the stove and said, "I love you and I'm going to fix chocolate chip cookies till they come out your ears!" She flew into Wayne's arms, and he held her so tightly that she dropped the cookie batter, which hardly mattered.

According to Barbara's friend, who told me this story, Barbara made no further complaints about her marriage.

An Unequal Partnership

Marriage works best as a partnership, but not necessarily an equal one. The way to have a sexually happy marriage is to put more than your half into the relationship. The happiness that doing so produces was shown by Marie and Eddie M. They were the envy of everyone who knew them. After ten years of marriage, Marie and Eddie still cuddled up together on a sofa at parties, held hands in public, and openly showed their affection for one another. One night at a dinner party the subject of marriage came up, and someone asked Marie for her secret. "It's no secret," she said, "just love. Only I don't just put half of the love into the marriage and wait for Eddie to supply the other half. I try to supply about eighty percent. And you know what?"

Eddie smiled and touched her hand. He said, "I'll tell you what. Her doing that makes me want to do the same thing. We get so busy doing for each other that we never stop to figure out who's doing the most."

Eddie and Marie had some tips, and I'll share them with you:

- *Tell of your love.* "I love you," is the most powerful sentence in the English language. Still, last week's "I love you" may have worn off by today. Repeat these magic words every day, three times a day as needed for happiness.

- *Show your love.* What could be sexier than showering someone with love? Every day, do something special for that special someone. Make it out of the ordinary—a flower or a note or a whispered promise—but make it special. To show your love.

● *Let love come naturally*. Spend time alone with your mate every day of the year. Devote this time to the two of you. Relax and let your love come naturally.

#2. Learn Your Mate's Sexual Needs and Respond to Them.

Sexual happiness comes naturally to some couples, but others have to invest love, understanding, and patience into building a mutually satisfying sex life. This is perfectly normal. Marriage itself is a beginning. A husband and wife who love each other can explore various techniques of lovemaking, can experiment with giving and receiving pleasure, can learn one another's sexual needs and respond to them.

What can happen when the husband doesn't understand the sexual needs of his wife can be shown by

Sue's Problem and the Unhappiness It Caused Her

Sue was a young married woman, and she came to the clinic because of nervousness. I prescribed a mild tranquilizer, but sensed the patient wanted to say something else. The nurse left the examining room, and Sue blurted out that she was sure she had a reason for her nervousness. "I've only been married three months," she said, "and my marriage is not turning out the way I thought it would."

Her problem was not all that uncommon. Sue had been raised right. She knew the basic facts about sex, but was a virgin until marriage. Her husband had also been a virgin. On their wedding night, the couple had sexual relations several times, and though Sue enjoyed the sex, she didn't like it as much as she'd hoped she would. She passed this off to her own inexperience, but in the three months since then, she'd never reached a sexual climax (orgasm). I explained to Sue that the goal in lovemaking need not be for the partners to reach a climax, but she was quick to point out that her husband always did. She was beginning to feel that sex was a one-sided affair and that it would remain that way. Her husband simply did not provide her with the kind of stimulation that she needed to enjoy sex. He'd seek and get his own pleasure, then finish the act and go to sleep.

I explained to Sue that her difficulty was not unusual among married people, and that by talking it out together, she and her husband could solve it. Sue did discuss it with her husband, and she had a surprise waiting for her. He admitted that he might have failed to meet her needs, but went on to say that she hadn't been meeting his needs. What may happen when a wife doesn't respond to her husband's desires can be shown by

Roger's Discovery of Why He Was a Poor Lover

Roger was Sue's husband. He admitted that he'd been neglecting to give his wife the stimulation she desired. I suggested some techniques he could use to arouse his wife, and as Roger listened, he realized something. "Say, you're naming the same things we used to do when we were courting. After we got married and started having sexual relations, I stopped spending much time on the preliminaries. I didn't know that Sue liked them and needed that warming up period so that she could enjoy the final act as much as I do."

Roger went on to make the comment that was an eye-opener for Sue. "You know," he said, "I guess one reason I'm not such a good lover any more is that some of the thrill's gone out of it. I expected sex to be the best thing in our marriage, but it hasn't been. Sue's not the same girl as when we were courting. She's too shy to let me watch her undress. By the time I see her she's got curlers in her hair and cold cream on her face. And she won't submit to anything until all the lights are out."

At this point, Sue said, "What difference could that possibly make?"

Roger smiled. "I don't know why I'm the way I am," he answered, "but not getting to see you does make a difference. I want to see all of you. Knowing that I can have your body is where I get a lot of my pleasure. And in the dark, it's just not the same."

Some Important Differences between Husband and Wife

Sue's and Roger's problem occurred because they didn't understand the differences in the way that a man and a woman respond to sexual stimulation. In the first place, the speed of response is not the same. A husband is ready much more quickly than is his wife. And, the sex partners become excited in different ways.

By making Roger keep the lights out, Sue was denying him a very enjoyable source of sexual stimulation. A husband likes to see his wife's body (just as many a wife enjoys viewing her husband's body). Seeing Sue parade by in see-through bikini panties and a low-cut bra might have turned Roger into a Casanova! Instead, Sue climbed into bed wearing hair curlers, and she made her husband turn out the lights before he touched her.

She didn't need the lights on to enjoy sex, but she did need more foreplay than she'd been getting. While they were courting, Sue and Roger had hugged and kissed for hours at a time. Roger had fondled Sue's breasts and squeezed her body and told her how much he loved her. These things excited Sue, but Roger stopped doing them after marriage. He wanted to go straight into the sex act, and Sue wasn't ready. She simply never caught up with his excitement, and just when *she* was beginning to be aroused *he* finished and withdrew.

Things a Man Can Do for a Woman

Roger met Sue's needs by changing his approach to their sexual relations. He stopped taking her love for granted, and began to woo her. She liked that, and to his surprise, so did Roger. Before they entered counseling, the couple had made it their practice to have sex the last thing at night, just before going to sleep. This was the only time when Sue was "ready." The house needed her attention during the early evening, then she took a bath and got out her clothes for the next day. She put her hair up in rollers while watching the late news, and patted cold cream onto her face before jumping into bed. Roger would turn out the lights and follow her. All this changed when Roger began to "seduce" his wife before bedtime.

Early in the evening he'd begin kissing her or nibbling on her ears. They'd embrace on the couch, and Roger would undress his wife. This was a sensual experience for both of them, since Sue also undressed Roger. Then, Roger would stroke Sue's body and whisper in her ear the way he had before they were married. He might give her a back rub, and slowly his hands would excite and arouse her. By the time they got around to going to the bedroom (and sometimes they didn't, preferring to have intercourse on the sofa), Sue was so excited she could barely contain herself. She had an orgasm the very first time her husband "seduced" her, and began enjoying sexual relations immensely.

Things a Woman Can Do for a Man

Sue responded to Roger by showing her willingness to change. She was naturally shy about her body, but grew to love her husband's instant reaction to her in the nude. In time, she accepted his seeing her that way as completely natural She stopped keeping Roger at bay when she was taking a bath, and at times they enjoyed the sensual experience of showering together. Best of all from Roger's standpoint, she purchased some sexy little underthings and began to wear them in front of him. She even learned to do a striptease. During their lovemaking, Sue turned the lights down low—but not out. The hair curlers? Well, Sue was a working woman and had to fix her hair. But she found that she could roll her hair and apply face cream the last thing before going to sleep.

#3. Learn to Receive Pleasure by Giving It.

The unique thing about love is that you have to give it away to get it! Still, the more you give, the more you get back in return. Giving can be pleasurable, and the enjoyment doubles when your mate returns the gift to you. The unfortunate fact is that some couples don't realize this. Early in marriage, for example, a man's sexual appetite may be so strong that he can think of little else but satisfying it. The wife, in turn, may come to feel that her body is for her husband's pleasure, and not for their mutual enjoyment. Sometimes a wife can feel so short-changed in the sexual relationship that she tries to give as little of herself as possible. I'm reminded of

The Woman Who Said "It's Bad Enough without Making It Any Worse"

Shirley W. was unhappy in her marriage, though this would have been difficult to tell from seeing her and her husband together. Shirley seemed to have everything. She was very attractive, as beautiful as a Miss America, and her husband, Frank, seemed devoted to her. A few years older than Shirley, Frank was a banker whose first wife had died in an auto accident. He and Shirley were very much in love, but when they returned from a honeymoon trip to Bermuda, it became apparent that they weren't getting along in all aspects of their married life.

Shirley phoned me one day to ask for advice. She wanted to know if every woman just tolerated sex like she did, or if some women actually enjoyed it. I assured her that a woman should enjoy lovemaking, but that it sometimes took some adjusting between the wife and husband. "Frank's just so . . . greedy," she said, her voice choking with emotion. "I know he loves me, but he takes me like he's ravenous and I'm a plate of food."

I spoke with Frank, and he admitted he was too hasty in his lovemaking. He said that he was very desirous of his wife, and that his haste was out of consideration for her. He sensed that Shirley wasn't enjoying intercourse, and he tried to get through the act as quickly as possible. Frank knew that this wasn't a solution, but he told himself that as time passed his wife's desire for sex might increase. For her part, Shirley wasn't helping the situation any. One thing she refused to do was remove all of her bedclothes during intercourse. Frank asked her why, and she said, "It's bad enough without making it any worse."

By solving the problem, Frank became

The Man Who Learned That Giving
Was the Sexiest Thing He Could Do

Frank set as his goal to try and give more pleasure to Shirley than he received from her. He went more slowly than before, and made an effort to learn the things that would arouse his wife. The deliberate approach worked. Shirley began to experience sexual feelings she didn't know she had. In turn, she began giving more. She discovered the fun of being an equal partner in lovemaking, and she and her husband began to enjoy an exciting love life! Frank learned that giving pleasure to his wife was the sexiest thing he could do.

The Gift of Love

Lovers exchange gifts, exchange kisses, exchange embraces. Happy are those who continue this giving relationship after marriage. The husband should learn his wife's needs and give her the stimulation she needs to stay abreast of his own sexual excitement. Doing so, he can't help but get more enjoyment out of lovemaking. The wife should realize that her full and unrestricted gift of love cannot but increase her own enjoyment of sex.

Here are some things to consider in your giving relationship:

- *Giving is pleasurable.* Let it come naturally, and ask only that your partner receive your gift.
- *Learn to receive pleasure.* Enjoy your partner's gift without feeling that you have to return it at that moment. Your enjoyment is a way of giving pleasure to the partner.
- *Discover the pleasure of saying "yes."* "Yes" is the sexiest word in the English language! Consider Molly Bloom's words at the end of the book *Ulysses* (her lover is her husband, Leopold Bloom): " . . . and then he asked me would I yes to say yes my mountain flower and first I put my arms around him yes and drew him down to me so he could feel my breasts all perfume yes and his heart was going like mad and yes I said yes I will Yes."[3] Give in and revel in the pleasure of "yes"!
- *Sex is only part of the giving of love.* A wife and husband can give to each other in so many ways! The beautiful thing is that every form of love expressed between husband and wife will increase their sexual joy. Intercourse at the climax of a day of giving can be a truly thrilling event!

#4. Be Aware That Sexual Love Can Take Many Forms.

The human being likes variety. What pleases you one day may not please you the next, and the same is true of your mate. Change is a fact of life, and it's a natural part of sexual growth. This should neither shock nor dismay you. Some couples are perfectly content to enjoy sexual intercourse in pretty much the same manner throughout their lives. Others find that variety adds spice, and that by experimenting with new methods they can keep their sexual relationship new and exciting and fun. Let me tell you about

---

[3] J. Joyce, *Ulysses*, Random House, New York, 1934, p. 768.

The Woman Who Added Variety—
and Zest—to Her Marriage

Ella M. was one of the most open, lovely women I've ever met. She was a psychiatric social worker at a place where I worked, and family and marital counseling came naturally to her. One day I accompanied her on a home visit, and listened with interest as she counseled a client on how to get more joy out of sex. "Freshen things up!" Ella said. "Get your hair fixed, get a different brand of perfume. Send the kids to the grandparents for the weekend. Buy yourself a new nightgown." The lady thought about the advice and said she didn't think it would work. Ella said, "All right. I'll tell you how to get his attention. Meet him at the door stark naked, and serve him his supper that way. That one is guaranteed to work." The client smiled conspiratorially, and I had the idea that her husband was in for a surprise that night.

"Do you really know those things will work?" I asked Ella after we left the client's house.

"Doctor," she said, "some people read books to learn that stuff. That's fine, but I've always felt I could write the book. Of course what I said will work. I've tried it out. Variety's the spice of life, and that's doubly true when you're speaking of sex. My husband and I—I don't mean to brag—but we have got just about the best and happiest marriage you could have. I told him something just after we got married, and he agreed completely. I said, 'Harry, if either of us changes, let's do it together.' Well, we've been married fifteen years and we've both changed, but in the same ways. And that's the reason we're happier right now than when we got married."

Ella and her husband proved that a lively imagination and a willingness to try new things can keep the sexual side of marriage the enjoyable activity that it should be. Later in this book I'll list some of the ways that a couple can express their love for each other in different forms. The thing to remember here is that *nothing that is mutually agreeable and satisfying between marriage partners need be considered wrong*. This may call for some readjustment in a husband's or wife's thinking. Well and good. The key words are "mutually agreeable and satisfying." When something pleases you and your mate, there's nothing wrong with doing it. You'd be rightfully angered if I took it on myself to list the things you and your mate should *not* do. Why? Because what happens between a husband and wife is none of my business. By the same token, don't let things you have heard or read shackle you from doing what you naturally want to do. Sexual happiness and sexual freedom go hand in hand.

In Chapters 5 and 6 I'll take up the many varieties of sexual love in describing the Sensual Union. Right now, it's time to take a closer look at sexual love between husband and wife. The next chapter is about sexual intercourse, and the following two chapters tell of a man's and a woman's roles in sexual love.

2

Sexual Intercourse: Total Love Between Two People

Sexual intercourse is a natural human function, and one doesn't have to be shown how to do it. On the other hand, expertise in making love must be acquired. Consider dancing. Almost anyone can move to music, but it takes skill to do the intricate steps and flourishes that set apart the expert from the beginner. You can learn about sexual intercourse from reading and hearing what others have to say, but in the end you and your mate must learn together the most pleasurable ways to make love. A certain amount of trial and error is inevitable during the first months of marriage. In time, you and your mate will develop the experience and confidence you need to satisfy one another's needs. Just remember that what pleases one couple may not be fun for you, and that the technique you and your partner like best may not rate number one in the books you read. But if both of you like it—do it!

The purpose of this chapter is to describe the four parts of the sex act, the main positions for intercourse, and the advantages and disadvantages of each position. First, however, let's make sure of the words we'll be using.

Some Terms to Know

I plan to use the following medical terms throughout this book:

Sexual Intercourse

1. Coitus (kō' it əs). This is another name for sexual intercourse, "sleeping together," or having sexual relations.
2. Orgasm (ôr' gaz'm). This is the height of sexual pleasure for a woman or a man. It also known as a climax, as "coming," or as "getting it."
3. Foreplay. This is the kissing, hugging and other stimulation that precede the insertion of the penis into the vagina. The excitement of foreplay is the first part of sexual intercourse.
4. Genital (jen' ə t'l). A person's sex organs are known as genital organs. Genitals and genitalia are related words.

The Wife's Parts

1. Vagina (və ji' nə). This is the woman's sex organ, the opening and passage into which the husband inserts his penis.
2. Vulva (vul' və). The parts around her vagina are a woman's vulva. These include the main lips, the small lips and the pubic hair.
3. Pubic hair. This is the mat of hair that covers the sensitive and fleshy area just above the main lips of the vulva.
4. Clitoris (klit' ər əs). A distinctly female organ, the clitoris is a small fleshy structure that lies in a fold of skin between the upper part of the main lips of the vulva. It is a very sensitive structure.

The Husband's Parts

1. Penis (pē' nis). This is the man's main sex organ. Sexual excitement causes it to enlarge, stand out from the body and become hard. The changes are known as *erection* (i-rek' shən). The head of the penis, or glans penis, is the enlarged tip end that has a velvety surface.
2. Testicles (tes'ti k'ls). Two round structures inside the bag, or

scrotum (skrōt' əm), the testicles are what make the man's sex hormones and produce the sperm that let him father a child.
3. Ejaculation (i-jak'-ye-lā'-shən). Fluid is released from a man's
penis when he has an orgasm. The fluid leaves the penis in spurts,
and the ejection of this *semen* (sē'-mən) is known as ejaculation, or
coming.

The Four Phases of Sexual Intercourse

A better understanding of sexual relations would not be possible without research. The most noteworthy research in this century
was done by Dr. Alfred C. Kinsey and his co-workers at the Insti-
tute for Sex Research, Indiana University. The work began in 1938,
and the book *Sexual Behavior in the Human Male* was published in
1948. In 1953 a companion volume, *Sexual Behavior in the Human
Female*, was published. The *Kinsey Report* was based on interviews
with thousands of people, and was an attempt to show the sexual
practices of average Americans. Two researchers at the Reproductive Biology Research Foundation, St. Louis, Missouri began in the
middle fifties to carry Kinsey's work a step further. They studied the
actual sexual response patterns of 382 women and 312 men between
the ages of 21 and 50. The two workers, Dr. William H. Masters
and Dr. Virginia E. Johnson (who are now married), published the
landmark book *Human Sexual Response* in 1966, and followed it
with *Human Sexual Inadequacy*, in 1970. Drs. Masters and Johnson
have shown that sexual intercourse actually consists of four phases.
These are:

1. *The excitement phase.*
2. *The plateau phase.*
3. *Orgasm.*
4. *Resolution.*

The four phases last varying lengths of time, and blend one
into the other. Also, they're not definitely correlated to when the
man puts his penis into the vagina. A woman, for example, may

reach her climax before insertion of the penis; so may a man. Nor does the excitement phase necessarily lead to orgasm. One of the marriage partners may not have an orgasm, or the couple may interrupt their lovemaking before either reaches a climax. One thing is certain. For either partner to have a satisfying sexual experience, he or she must first become sexually excited.

1. The Excitement Phase.

The excitement phase is characterized by the giving and receiving of pleasure. It begins with an "I'm in the mood" signal from one or the other of the sex partners. Maybe the wife will show a part of her body to the husband, almost accidentally, but letting him get the message. Or, he may begin stroking and fondling her. Men tend to become excited more quickly than women, but this isn't always the case. Still, *the husband should be aware that as a rule, his wife will build to a peak of excitement more slowly than he will, and that she can become sexually aroused by stimulation of almost any part of her body.* A loving husband can become a great lover just by remembering this simple fact. The happiness that a thorough excitement phase brings to a woman can be shown by the case of

The Wife Who Said, "I Never Knew It Could Be Like That."

Joyce W. was an attractive woman in her early thirties. She'd been divorced and was happily remarried, and I heard her speak at a seminar on the woman's role in sexual expression. Many of the women who spoke at this conference were angry, and with reason. They were frustrated because their husbands (or former husbands, in many cases) didn't or hadn't understood their sexual needs. One of the main points they made was that the arousal phase of sex relations was just as enjoyable as the remainder of the act. "I enjoy arousal almost more than the final act," Joyce W. said, "and it's taken me into my thirties and two marriages to learn it. But learn it I did! My first husband and I rarely had enjoyable sex, at least for me, but my present husband knows what I like. I'll never forget our wedding night! He made love to me, to *all* of me. Of course our physical relations were tied in with our love for one another, but even so, it was something else. I remember snuggling into my pillow afterwards and just floating in space. Then I leaned over and whispered to him that I never knew it could be like that. It was one of the happiest moments of my life."

Ways of Generating Sexual Excitement

● *A husband* can excite his wife by learning the sensitive parts of her body and paying attention to them. A woman's eyes, ears and mouth are sensitive. One woman told me that her husband didn't discover until several years after they were married that her ears were her most sensitive spot. "But I guess it's just as well," she confided. "If he'd known about my ears before we got married, my first child might be a year older than he is."

Her legs, arms, back and tummy are tingly areas of a woman's body. Her breasts, fingertips, palms and feet are exquisitely sensitive to arousal—and so are her thighs and genital parts.

● *A wife* can excite her husband just by letting him see a part of her that isn't usually visible. Sight of his wife's thighs, breasts or totally nude body may bring on a husband's erection. A man's excitement rises even higher when his wife spends some time arousing him. Especially enjoyable is stimulation of his penis or the skin around it. The stimulation need not be by hand or fingers every time. A wife can rub with her body. She can touch a breast to the penis, or squirm around during an embrace, or massage a man's front with her backside.

The man and woman should alternate giving and receiving pleasure. There need be no definite pattern, but changing roles is pleasurable for both partners. The excitement phase may continue for a few minutes to several hours, and can lead into the other phases of intercourse or be broken off when either or both partners want to stop temporarily and continue later. Indeed, some couples find it exciting to arouse one another for a couple of days before on the third day actually completing the act of lovemaking.

2. The Plateau Phase.

If sexual stimulation continues, the husband and wife will enter the plateau phase. By this time the couple are usually undressed and in bed or lying on a soft surface. The woman's vagina is moist and receptive, the man's penis erect and throbbing. He may enter her and initiate the thrusting motions of sexual intercourse. Or she may mount him, and guide the penis into her vagina. Each person's breathing becomes heavy and quick. The heart beats faster. Both partners become aware of a tingling, very good feeling in the sex organs.

Ordinarily, the plateau phase is fairly brief, and the drive to get still more enjoyment leads into the next phase, orgasm. However, the husband and wife may not reach the plateau phase at the same time, or either or both of them can still withdraw from sexual stimulation and not have an orgasm.

3. Orgasm.

The orgasm is the sexual climax, the peak of feeling that caps off all that's come before. It is the absolute height of human sensation, and it brings with it an outpouring of semen from the man, and of physical and emotional tension from both partners. A man's climax lasts about 3-12 seconds. A woman's may be felt for this long or longer. As a matter of fact, the wife can have many orgasms, one right after another, though she is usually satisfied having several or just one.

4. The Resolution Phase.

This is the time when the man and woman return to normal after the physical and emotional outpouring of a climax. They relax, savor the experience, and tell one another of their love. A woman can recover rapidly from the resolution phase and have additional orgasms if she is stimulated to do so. A man, by contrast, can't continue until after a period of time lasting at least 10 or 15 minutes, and perhaps as long as a day or a week. However, a man's penis doesn't wilt instantly after his ejaculation. It stays hard for a time. He can and should use it to let his wife enjoy her more gradual resolution phase. At times, she will reach orgasm while her husband is going through the resolution phase. A man named Herbert learned to give his wife the satisfaction she wanted, but until then she was

The Woman Who Never Quite Got There

Edna and Herbert had been married for years, and described their sex as "usually enjoyable." Lately, though, Edna's interest had declined. She had stopped having orgasms, and was disappointed and frustrated. She asked her husband to spend longer on foreplay, and he did. Nevertheless, once Herbert entered the plateau phase, he progressed rapidly to a climax. Afterwards he stopped his thrusting movements, and his wife didn't get the stimulation she needed to achieve sexual fulfillment.

Finally, Edna mentioned to Herbert that if he could continue for just a little longer after his climax, it would be great for her. The next time they made love, Herbert did just that. He went as slowly as he could through the stages before orgasm. After his ejaculation, he held his hard penis inside his wife and continued to make the motions of intercourse. Within a minute or two, Edna reached a climax. She was so pleased and grateful to Herbert that she began pleading with him to make love to her more often. Herbert felt like pinching himself for not thinking of this simple technique much earlier.

At times, every husband will need to perform this way. An

erection may persist for several minutes after ejaculation, and it's nothing more than good manners—and expert lovemaking technique—to continue thrusting motions until the wife has reached her climax.

The Positions for Sexual Intercourse

Imaginative couples have made love on a roller-coaster, a Ferris wheel, a motorcycle, even in the front seat of a small airplane, which I presume was on automatic pilot. At times, you and your mate may like to have intercourse in the shower stall, the front seat of your automobile or under the kitchen table. It's true that sexual intercourse can be performed just about anywhere, but the time and place of the event may dictate the method. Actually, there are only six main positions for intercourse, and the others are variations of these. The six positions are:

1. Man on top.
2. Woman on top.
3. Side by side.
4. Rear entry.
5. Sitting.
6. Standing.

The main reason for knowing the different positions is not necessarily that you'll choose to use all of them or even try them out. You may be perfectly content with one position and not want to change. However, varying the position for intercourse can keep it the new and exciting event that it should be.

1. Man on Top.

This is the most common position for lovemaking in America and Europe. It's known as the "missionary" position, and some people consider it the only normal position for sexual intercourse. Such persons are wrong. Any position that the couple finds mutually pleasurable is normal. Dr. Kinsey found that almost all the couples he surveyed used this position most frequently, but went on to point out that in Asia, Africa and other parts of the world other positions are used regularly. In fact, as the authors of a book by and for women have pointed out, the missionary position got its name because natives of certain foreign countries had never used it until a missionary told them to.[1]

● *THE POSITION.* The man takes a position on top of his wife or kneels between her legs as she rests on her back. By opening her thighs and bending her knees, the wife makes it easy for her husband to insert his penis. She needn't keep her legs in this position throughout coitus, and she may find that resting her hips on a pillow will make her more comfortable.

● *Variations.* The man can hold all his weight on his elbows, palms and knees, or let his body rest full-length against his wife. By lifting his legs, the husband can let his wife close her thighs beneath him. She can exert a pleasant squeezing action on his penis and testicles—and have more control over the rate and depth of intercourse. Variations are possible when the husband's knees are between his wife's legs. She can lift her feet and encircle her husband's waist with her legs. Or, she can lift her legs even higher so that the backs of her knees come to rest on her husband's shoulders.

● *Advantages* of this position include the fact that it's acceptable to most couples. The wife can relax and be receptive to her husband's caresses. The position is a good one for the woman who wants to become pregnant; after ejaculation, her husband's semen tends to remain in the vagina. (But pregnancy can occur after intercourse in any position!) For a man, this position seems to satisfy a basic urge to dominate and possess his wife. Certainly the man has the most room to maneuver, and to control the rate of lovemaking.

● *Disadvantages* are that the position restricts the woman and places a strain on the man. The wife may feel pinned down, which she is. She's not able to move very well, and thus may tend to take a passive role. Women who've never had intercourse in any but this position are less likely to have orgasms than are women who have coitus in other positions. A relative disadvantage of the position is

---

[1]The Boston Women's Health Book Collective, *Our Bodies, Ourselves,* Simon and Schuster, New York, 1971, p. 34.

that it tends to bring a man rapidly to a climax. (He might not object, but his wife might if she remained unsatisfied.) Finally, the position is not good for late in pregnancy, when the wife's tummy is large, and it can be uncomfortable for a wife when her husband is obese.

2. Woman on Top.

This is a natural position for sexual intercourse, and on a country by country basis it may be the most popular coital position in the world. Certainly it is the preferred position for women who have used it. Kinsey found that only a third of American women born before 1900 had ever used this position. Over half of women born between 1920 and 1929 had used the position, and probably the frequency is much higher among women born since 1950.

● *THE POSITION.* It is just the reverse of the man on top position; the husband and wife swap places. He rests on his back, with or without his buttocks supported by a pillow. By kneeling or sitting above her husband, the wife can guide the penis into her vagina. (In every position, the wife is the one who should guide the penis into the vagina; she's simply better able to do this than her husband.) She can support her weight on her knees and legs, sit on her husband's thighs, or stretch out on top of him.

● *Variations.* The woman can keep her knees to the outside of her husband's legs and allow deep penetration, or she can keep her thighs together once the penis is inserted and thus control the depth of intercourse. The man can bend his knees and caress his wife's body with his thighs. It's possible for the couple to begin intercourse with the man on top, and then roll into the woman on top position. She can then sit up or kneel over him. Changing positions during coitus can be fun, and you and your mate may discover an especially pleasurable variation of a standard position.

● *Advantages.* Sitting or kneeling over her husband gives the wife great freedom of movement. Deep penetration of the vagina is possible, yet the wife can control the rate of intercourse. She can make to-and-fro thrusts, move side to side, or rotate her hips in a clockwise or counterclockwise motion. At the same time, her husband's hands are free to fondle her breasts, buttocks, thighs and vulva. The man is less likely to have a quick climax than when he is on top, while his wife's excitement will progress more rapidly. Indeed, many women who can't reach a climax when a man is above can do so easily—and repetitively—by taking the topmost position. Finally, the woman on top position may be a great boost for the wife's morale. She may lose many of her inhibitions and enjoy sex more. An example of the benefits of this position can be shown by

The Woman Who Discovered a Way to Sexual Happiness

Margie, a 41-year-old mother of three, had never enjoyed sex as much as she felt she should. She longed to feel the same thrill as her husband, but in all their years of lovemaking she had never reached a climax. She'd begun to wonder if she ever would.

On a weekend trip with two other women to a large city, Margie went to an X-rated movie. The couple in the movie made love in many positions, most of them new to Margie. After the movie the three women began to discuss sex, and Margie learned that her two friends had made love in the woman on top position. Margie made some plans of her own. Next time she and her husband had intercourse, she said, "Wait a minute. Let me show you something." She then mounted him and had the first climax of her life. Margie's husband was very pleased. He told her that her discovery of the new position was the best thing that ever happened to their sex life.

● *Disadvantages*. Because it permits deep penetration, the position can be painful if the wife has a tender ovary or womb. It's not a good position when the couple are trying to cause a pregnancy, since the man's semen tends to flow out of the vagina. Nor is this a good position when the woman's tummy is large from pregnancy. The main drawback to the position may be the husband's hesitation in accepting it. A wife should understand that her husband's sexuality is composed of many things. He sees himself as his wife's protector and provider, the leader in their partnership. His ability to have an erection can be lost temporarily if he's put in a passive role in lovemaking. Still, most husbands will accept the position when they realize that it will add to the wife's sexual pleasure. The couple may begin intercourse with the man on top, then go to the woman on top position. After the wife has a climax or is near one, the couple can change positions so that the man is uppermost for the remainder of intercourse. Love, understanding, and a willingness to give will let the couple get the most out of this position.

3. Side by Side.

The side-by-side position has equality going for it (neither partner is on top), and it is a restful position that will let the couple have intercourse as rapidly or slowly as they wish.

● *THE POSITION.* The easiest way to get into the side-by-side position is to start out with the wife on her back and the man above her. He places both knees between her thighs, inserts his penis, and rolls to one side or the other. The wife can then adjust her bottommost leg so that it isn't caught under his weight. A comfortable position is for her to gently encircle his waist with her thighs.

● *Variations.* The man can keep his legs on the outside of his wife's body as they begin the position, so that when they roll over, the weight of her lower body will rest on one of his thighs. Of course, the position can be taken on two different sides, which in itself allows variation. Finally, though the couple remain face to face, they can press their upper bodies together or remain at arm's length for better caressing and fondling during intercourse.

● *Advantages.* This position lets the husband and wife share the movements of intercourse. Both partners have their hands free.

The position is restful, and is well-suited to the man or woman bothered by arthritis or another medical condition. Some experts believe that this is the ideal position for intercourse during the first days and weeks of marriage.

● *Disadvantages.* The side-by-side position doesn't work very well when the husband or wife is obese, or late in pregnancy when the tummy may get in the way.

4. Rear Entry.

● *THE POSITION.* The husband takes a position behind his wife and inserts the penis into the vagina from the rear. Most commonly they are reclining side by side, but many variations are possible.

● *Variations.* The wife can kneel on her hands and knees, rest her knees on the floor and her upper body on the bed, or rest on her stomach as her husband enters her. She can keep her thighs spread or close them over her husband's genitals. Deeper penetration is possible when the wife draws her thighs up and the husband moves his upper body back and his lower body forward until he is almost perpendicular to his wife.

● *Advantages.* Because the wife has no fear of pressure on her stomach, rear entry is an excellent position for intercourse during the latter part of pregnancy. It's also a relaxing method of lovemaking when one partner is ill or unable to take a more active role in coitus. The man may enjoy pressing against his wife's buttocks. Also, his hands are free to reach out and encircle or caress her body during intercourse.

● *Disadvantages* include that the woman may object to rear entry. Some wives find it distasteful—so do some husbands! A woman is more likely to object to the rear entry position because it gives very little stimulation to the clitoris. Other couples dislike the fact that the position keeps them from facing one another during lovemaking. Rear entry isn't for the obese man or the man whose penis is small.

5. Sitting.

● *THE POSITION*. The man sits on the edge of the bed, in a chair, or on the floor, while his wife takes a position astride him.

● *Variations*. The woman can turn so that she is facing away from her husband—in effect, a rear entry position. Or, the wife can sit on the edge of the bed, spread her legs, and let her husband kneel between them. He may need a cushion beneath his knees to achieve the right height for insertion.

● *Advantages*. The sitting position adds variety to lovemaking. Some couples unable to have intercourse in another position may accomplish it this way. It's a good method for an obese woman, or one who is very pregnant.

● *Disadvantages* are that some couples find this position objectionable, while others don't get much satisfaction from it. Neither partner may feel relaxed, and the lack of body contact removes an important source of arousal.

6. Standing.

● *THE POSITION*. A husband and wife who are about the same height can have intercourse while standing and facing one another. The wife must spread her thighs to allow insertion, and the man may have to bend his knees and bring the lower part of his trunk forward.

● *Variations*. The woman may lock her arms around her husband's neck and lift her legs so that they encircle his waist. This can be tiring on the man. The woman could rest her weight on the edge of the dressing table, but then the position becomes a variation of the sitting position. Rear entry while the couple is standing is also possible.

● *Advantages*. The standing position can please both partners, and it is adaptable to many locations. The couple can have relations in a shower, lake, swimming pool—or small closet. Once a husband and wife have lost their shyness about each other, they may enjoy standing and having intercourse in front of a mirror—at least during part of the love act.

• *Disadvantages* are that the position may be tiring and isn't meant for couples who differ greatly in height. A potential problem is that at the moment of climax one or both partners may lose control, stumble and fall.

Developing New Positions Together

The tendency for a newly married couple is to experiment with new positions, find several that are mutually pleasurable, and then settle down to use one of these for the rest of their married life. According to Dr. John E. Eichenlaub, author of *The Marriage Art*, precisely the opposite course makes more sense. The husband and wife might do well to develop mutually satisfying relations in one or two positions, and then branch out to explore other positions. One thing is certain. The couple who would turn their sex into an acrobatic performance are missing the point. Love is giving, and the goal is mutual pleasure. What can happen when gymnastics begin to dominate was shown by

The Man Who Went Too Far Too Fast

James W., a 43-year-old man, read a book about lovemaking techniques, and told his wife that they had been missing out on good sex for years and years. Jim's wife, Frieda, disagreed. She liked their sex just the way it was. They always had intercourse in the man on top position, and though Frieda didn't climax every time, she found sex pleasurable and interesting. Jim nevertheless insisted that she try new positions. Reluctantly, Frieda did so. She didn't like the rear entry position, and felt silly in the woman on top position. She asked Jim if they could go back to their old practices; he very pointedly suggested that she see a doctor. Frieda talked over the disagreement with her physician, who said that sex should be fun—

for both partners. Jim and Frieda ended up by compromising. He stopped asking her to have sex in positions she didn't like, while she agreed to open up their lovemaking by trying some of the new things Jim suggested. By developing new techniques together, Jim and Frieda began to enjoy a better sex life.

Most sexually happy couples do use several positions for intercourse, either at different times or during one lovemaking session. The positions need not be used in the same order or in exactly the same way any two times in a row. The key word for developing new positions is *together*. Do what you like, provided both of you like it. The important thing is that you and your mate experiment together and take your time. A woman may not feel comfortable in the top position until she's been married for five or ten years, nor may a man want to relinquish the top position during the first years of marriage. Again, no two couples are the same. Do what works for you. Sexual intercourse is a way of saying "I love you," and the feelings that accompany the act are much more important than how the act is performed.

Length of Intercourse

Some couples have longer lovemaking sessions than others. Most of the variation in the time that it takes to have intercourse occurs during the excitement phase. Studies have shown that after a man inserts his penis into the vagina, he'll reach a climax and have an ejaculation within 1-5 minutes (average = 3 minutes). The man will average about 30-50 frictional movements of his penis in the vagina before having his climax.

In years past, many physicians felt that a woman needed a long lovemaking session to have an orgasm. More important than the duration of intercourse, however, is the degree of arousal of the two partners. A man who's expert at arousing his wife may find that she has an orgasm soon after he enters her. A man who doesn't give his wife the stimulation she needs may find that she's dissatisfied even after 20 or 30 minutes of intercourse. In *The Hite Report*, Shere Hite summarized the views of women about lengthy intercourse.[2] Some women reported that long intercourse caused soreness or a burning feeling afterwards when urinating. More than one woman said that the most enjoyable part of intercourse was when the man inserted his penis, and that subsequent movements were less pleasurable.

It's reasonable to say that 30 minutes or an hour should be set aside for a lovemaking session. Passionate and fulfilling intercourse can be accomplished in 5 minutes for that matter, but it would be unusual for this to be the case time after time. The husband and wife who take the time to set the mood and to love and respond to one another will reap the benefit of greater sexual satisfaction.

Frequency of Sexual Intercourse

The Kinsey Report revealed that couples who were less than 25 years old had relations an average of two to four times a week, but the frequency had dropped to about once a week by age forty. Still, some couples reported having intercourse every day into their fifties; a few couples in their forties had sexual relations four times a day, every day of the week.

A man reaches the peak of his sexual abilities in his late teens and early twenties. Thereafter, he experiences a steady decline in sex drive. A woman, by contrast, may start her sex life with less urgency. Over the years of marriage, however, her inhibitions tend to leave and she may get more pleasure out of sex. She may not reach her peak of sexual capabilities until her thirties, and may maintain a high level of sexual interest right on up into her sixties. One woman in her forties told me in a terse whisper that she was afraid her husband didn't love her any more. I asked why. She said that during the last few months he had stopped making love to her every night, and was now favoring an every other night frequency. I explained the differences between sexual desires in a man and a

---

[2]Shere Hite, *The Hite Report*, Macmillan Pub. Co., New York, 1976, p. 185.

woman, and pointed out that the quality of lovemaking was just as important as the quantity. In fact, some couples find that making love less frequently can heighten the enjoyment when they have intercourse.

The frequency of sexual relations is something each husband and wife must establish on their own. They'll find that the frequency will vary. Some weeks are sexier than others. Going on a trip together may stir up simmering passions. Illness of one marital partner will reduce the frequency of relations. Some women want sex near the time of the menstrual period, others don't. Some women experience a strong urge for intercourse at the time of ovulation, about halfway between menstrual periods. The bottom line is that husbands and wives should enjoy sexual intercourse as often as they wish. It is a way of communication that soars above the ordinary. We'll take up some lovemaking techniques in the next two chapters, as we look in detail at the man's and the woman's roles in sexual love.

3

The Man's Role in
Sexual Love

*B*y tradition, the man is the aggressor in sexual relations. He asks a woman for dates, asks her to go steady, and asks for her hand in marriage. This traditional man-woman relationship is based on the fact that a woman is the one who becomes pregnant. She doesn't want to have a baby until the right time, and thus can't offer herself to just any man who comes along. On the other hand, sexual relations between a married couple are perfectly natural. A man can still take the lead, or he can let his wife set the pace of lovemaking. The important thing is that he does what is comfortable and what he and his wife want to do.

The purpose of this chapter is to tell about a man's sexuality and the things that turn him on; to describe his sex organs and their response to excitement; and to show the man's response to sexual intercourse. An awareness of these things will give the man a better understanding of how he can get more out of sex.

A Man's Sexuality

A man has distinct features that every woman recognizes. He talks in a deep voice, has a beard (whether or not he shaves) and tends to be more forward and aggressive than a woman. A man owes his development and personality to chemical changes that occur in his body. The man's sex hormone, *testosterone*, causes his penis and testicles to grow, and makes it possible for him to ejaculate (release semen) at the peak of his sexual excitement. The hormone also stimulates his sex drive and causes him from the age of adolescence onward to take a keen interest in girls.

Puberty: A Time of Change

The changes that make a man a man begin before he is born, and at birth his penis and testicles are completely formed. A male infant can have an erection, but his penis doesn't begin to grow until puberty. Then, his testicles secrete testosterone in large amounts, and the hormone circulates through his body to produce growth and change. The boy's chest and shoulders get bigger, he grows taller, and his sex organs mature. He takes an interest in girls, and finds himself wanting to kiss and embrace a member of the opposite sex. The man's sexuality has begun, and it will continue for the rest of his life.

Most young men are not nearly as successful in their sexual exploits as they would have other young men or women believe. The chief form of sexual relief is masturbation—self-stimulation. The act is completely natural for a man, and is performed by the overwhelming majority of them. The reason a sexual outlet is so important to a young man is that his sexual urges reach a peak relatively early in his life. His drives are as strong during his late teens and early twenties as they will ever be. Even so, his sex organs continue to grow from the time of puberty (around age 13) until he's in his early twenties.

The Penis

The penis is the main sex organ of a man, and it has the unique ability to get bigger when the man becomes sexually excited. The enlargement, known as erection, occurs when more blood flows into the penis than can be carried away by the circulation. The effect is to blow the penis up like air pumps up a balloon. The organ may almost double in size.

The average length of a mature man's penis when it is in its unerect state is about three inches—the length of his index finger. The average length of the erect penis is six inches, and it is an inch and a half in diameter. As a rule, the larger a man's sex organ when it is limp, the less it will increase in size during an erection. A man whose unerect penis is only two and a half inches long, for example, may have an erect penis that is five inches long. By the same token, a man whose limp penis is three and a half inches long may have an erect penis that is five and a half inches long.

It's natural for a man to have some doubts about the size of his penis. He may have glanced around while showering with a group of men and noticed that his organ wasn't as big as that of some of the other men. The thing a man should realize is that his wife's vagina is just right for his penis. A woman is far less impressed with big size than most men believe, and some women find that intercourse is more enjoyable when the man's penis is just a little below average in size. The reason is that much of a woman's satisfaction comes from stimulation of her clitoris, a small organ located above her vagina in some skin folds inside the main lips of the vulva. Intercourse accomplished by a small penis is just as effective in stimulating the clitoris as is intercourse with a large penis.

How a man feels about the size of his penis is more important than its actual measurement. If he believes that it's a desirable size, he'll be able to perform for his wife like a champion lover. She is the one best able to judge size, and ought to brag about her husband's penis and tell him how much she likes it. Nothing can make a man feel sexier than his wife's genuine praise! By contrast, even the slightest negative reaction may be misinterpreted by the man and may cause him to have difficulties. This can be shown by the case of

The Woman Who Laughed at the Wrong Time

Joy W. came in for sexual counseling. Her husband, Bill, had lost interest in having sex with her. Joy suspected he might be having an affair, and wanted to know what she could do to make herself more appealing to her husband.

Their problem began one night several months previously, when they were about to have sexual intercourse. The phone rang and Joy went to answer it. When she returned, her husband's erection was gone. He was unable to regain it, and Joy laughed at his predicament. Bill took it the wrong way. For one thing, he'd always suspected that his penis was smaller than average. He interpreted his wife's laughter as ridicule at his inadequacy. His inability to perform led to self-doubt. His next few attempts to have sex with his wife failed, and then he stopped trying. Bill hadn't been having an affair, but he was terribly concerned by what he called "my failure as a man."

By talking out his problem, Bill was able to see that what had happened to him was no indication he'd lost his manhood. I explained that many men have had a similar episode. The problem, of course, was that Joy had laughed at the wrong time. Still, she didn't think Bill's penis was small. She thought it was just right. Her laughter had been the natural reaction of one who's a little embarrassed and not certain what to do. Joy profited by the experience. She learned to take a patient and understanding role in their sexual relations, and soon she and Bill were once again enjoying a happy sex life.

Key to a Man's Heart

Joy and Bill might not have had their problem if Joy had realized that a man's view of himself has everything to do with his performance as a lover. In fact, the key to his heart is his brain. He wants to please his wife, to show off for her and be in her eyes the most desirable and exciting creature in the world. She and she alone can give him the praise that he needs to feel good about himself.

"J," author of *The Sensuous Woman*, wrote that a man is really the weaker of the sexes. He comes on strong and aggressive, but beneath the surface he's a little boy who wants to do well and earn the praise that only a wife can give him. Marabel Morgan, writing in *The Total Woman*, made the point that a middle-aged man looking in the mirror doesn't see a middle-aged man. He sees the same clean-cut, attractive boy he has always been. Wise is the wife who sees also this image when she looks at her husband.

Sexual Stimulation in a Man

A woman is physically capable of having sex at any time of the day or night, but a man is different. He cannot directly will his penis to undergo the changes necessary for intercourse. Erection is a reflex that is mediated through the involuntary nervous system, and the right emotional signals must reach the brain before the reflex goes into action. What happens is this: Signals pour into the man's brain and set off nerve impulses that run down his spinal cord. The impulses bring a surge of blood flowing into his penis. An erection occurs. The reaction takes only a few seconds, provided the man is healthy, emotionally in tune, and receives the right signals at the right time. Some of the things that can cause a man to have an erection are:

- *Thinking sexy thoughts.*
- *Seeing a sexy picture or movie.*
- *Sight of a woman's body or undergarments.*
- *Kissing, embracing or fondling a woman's body.*
- *Having his body stimulated by a woman.*

What He Thinks Is Important

Women and men share the fact that they can become sexually excited just by thinking sexy thoughts. However, a man's sexual excitement usually comes more speedily than his wife's. Just one thought may bring on an erection, and in scarcely more than a second or two. A boy in his teens may have so many sexy thoughts accompanied by erections that he finds himself wishing he could get his mind on something else. He can't, at least not for very long. Seeing himself as the hero in erotic fantasies prepares the young man for playing this role to his wife. Nor do the fantasies stop after marriage. The man may continue to have them right on up into his fifties, sixties and seventies. The point is, a husband's seeming suddenness in his sexual approach to his wife may not seem sudden to him. He may have been carrying a little fantasy around in his mind all day. She was probably the star performer, and he can't wait to make his dream come true.

Sex on Sight: Instant Erection

Few things can turn a man on more quickly than the sight of a woman's nude body. This is why certain moviemakers and magazine publishers have made a fortune. Many persons find pornography repulsive, but it couldn't exist unless people paid for it, and men tend to be the best customers. Nature made the human male the way he is, and most men would prefer to see the real item instead of a picture. A wife can take advantage of this by letting her own body be the focus of the man's attention. If he gets pleasure from seeing her, she should let him. The wife who hides her body from her husband runs the risk of turning him into someone like

The Man Who Kept Peeking Through the Bathroom Door

Dahlia D. was raised in a strict household. Her parents never showed affection in front of the children, and each family member was required to be completely clothed when in view of the others. After her marriage to Alberto, Dahlia continued to act in the same formal way that she had learned from her parents. Alberto was different. He was deeply in love with his wife, and longed to see her body as well as make love to her. His wife's modesty was puzzling to Alberto. She wouldn't let him undress her, and she wouldn't let him see her in the nude. In fact, she kept on part of her bedclothes when they made love, and insisted that the act be performed in the dark.

One night while Dahlia was taking a bath, she thought she saw a man peeking through the bathroom door. It was Alberto. Wearing a big grin and nothing else, he stalked toward the tub for some love play. Dahlia was angered rather than excited, and she hurt her husband's feelings. He got over that and soon they'd resumed what for them was a normal sex life. However, Dahlia soon realized that her husband was turning into something of a peeping tom. He loved to invent excuses to come into the bathroom while she was using it, and sometimes he'd peep through the crack of the door to stare at her.

Dahlia was so upset by Alberto's behavior that she reported it to the doctor. He explained that Alberto was probably a man who got turned on more by seeing his wife than by feeling her body in bed after the lights were out. The physician thought that Alberto's behavior, though unusual, was simply his normal response to his wife's modesty. He advised Dahlia to be more open with her love.

People don't change overnight, but once Dahlia understood the reason for Alberto's behavior, she stopped denying him the pleasure of seeing her. She discovered that giving Alberto what he wanted gave her pleasure, and this helped take away her embarrassment at being nude in front of him. A few months later she reported to her doctor that she and Alberto had made a satisfactory adjustment. Alberto didn't look through the bathroom door any more. They had just moved to a house with a large shower, and were showering together every morning before work!

Little Things Count

A wife need not parade through the bedroom *au naturel* to turn her husband on, because giving him a glimpse of her breasts or hips will accomplish the same thing. Little things count. The way a woman undresses, the way she covers or reveals parts of her body, the way she unties and combs her hair—all these things can excite her husband. Smell is also important.

A 45-year-old man told me that he got an instant erection when he smelled a certain perfume that his wife wore. It was an exotic fragrance, and she made a habit of wearing just the right amount of it in just the right places when she was in just the right mood. This wife knew exactly what she was doing! She'd discovered a sexy and provocative way of turning her husband on and announcing her own readiness for sex.

Sensitive Spots

Kissing and embracing excite a man, and so does the stimulation of certain parts of his body. A wife should learn her husband's sensitive spots, just as he should learn hers. I'll list the woman's erogenous zones in the next chapter, and discuss the male sensitive spots here.

Male Erogenous Zones

Every part of a man's body is sensitive to his wife's touch. However, certain parts are more sensitive than others. In addition, stimulation of a certain place on one man's body may create an exquisitely pleasurable sensation; stimulation of the same spot on another man's body may evoke no reaction. Here, in approximate order of sensitivity, is a list of the male erogenous zones.

- The penis
- The scrotum and anus
- The mouth
- The ears
- The nipples
- Palms and fingertips
- Armpits
- The lower belly
- The chest
- The back and hips

The Penis: Top of the List

His sex organ is the most sensitive part of a man's body. A wife can stimulate the penis in many ways, but she should understand that parts of the organ are more sensitive than others, and that direct stimulation of the penis may bring her husband to orgasm before the onset of intercourse. The most sensitive part of the penis is its head, called the *glans penis*.

The Glans

"Glans" is Latin for acorn, and the glans does resemble an acorn. In a limp organ it is pink and rather small, but it doubles in size and turns almost purple during an erection. Its texture is different from that of regular skin. It has a velvety surface, and is studded with nerve endings. It's also softer than the rest of the organ, and the softness serves as a pad to make entrance of the penis into the vagina a gentle, pleasurable sensation. The web-like cord beneath the front tip of the glans is the *frenulum* (Latin word for bridle). It is an especially sensitive area.

Openings near the glans secrete a cheesy substance called smegma. It has two purposes. Smegma keeps the glans moist, and gives off a sexual scent. Most women find the smell stimulating, so long as the man is clean and the rest of his body is alluring.

The glans stand out as the most obvious part of a man's erect penis. However, it may not be visible in the limp penis of an uncircumcised man. The reason for this is that men are born with a sheath of skin that covers the glans. Circumcision is the operation that removes this skin. Most men born in the U.S. since World War II have had the operation, but men who have not been circumcised are just as normal (or more so) than those who have been.

A man performs masturbation by moving the skin of his penis back and forth over the glans. He may prefer to rub the skin slowly with one or two fingers, or he may grasp the entire penis and pump the skin up and down vigorously. A wife can imitate these motions and give her husband pleasure. However, she should realize that stimulating the glans penis in this manner may bring the man rapidly to orgasm.

The Woman Who Turned the Right
Knob Too Often

Sally married in her late thirties, and enjoyed sex tremendously. To make her sex life even more enjoyable, she began to read about various ways to excite her husband, Richard. One way was to stimulate his penis in the same way he might use to masturbate. Sally tried this and Richard liked it. In fact, he enjoyed her gift so much that he ejaculated and was unable to have intercourse with her. The same thing happened the next night, and the next. Sally was a little disappointed the third time, and she whispered to Richard that she wanted to give him pleasure, but not so much that he couldn't complete their lovemaking.

"I don't start out wanting you to do that," he said, "but once you begin it's so good I can't ask you to stop." Richard concluded by saying, "Let's spend our time the next few nights on how to please *you*."

By focusing most of their foreplay on Sally, the couple were able to return to having mutually pleasurable sexual intercourse. Perhaps the question Sally should have asked herself was not how she could excite Richard, but whether he needed much in the way of additional stimulation. In many ways, the duration of excitement for a man is more important than the degree of excitement. He'll enjoy sex more if he can extend the excitement phase of intercourse for 20-30 minutes, and by then his wife will have time to build up to her own peak of excitement. By confining her caresses to his less sensitive areas, a wife can keep her husband from reaching orgasm too soon.

Other Parts, Other Responses

Early in marriage, a man may not need or want much stimulation from his wife. However, the man who does enjoy this or who needs it to achieve an erection will respond to fondling of various parts of his body. These are the reactions his wife might expect:

- *Tweaking the nipples* or touching them lightly will cause them to erect. They'll sprout goosebumps and become hard, and the man's penis may also become erect if it hasn't already. Some men flinch at the touch of their nipples, and would rather be touched on another body part.
- *A man's mouth and ears* are sensitive to his wife's touch. She can do the touching with her fingers, her lips, her

tongue or a breast. The breast is excellent for caressing, and the stimulation may excite the woman as much as the man.

- *Touching his armpits* can arouse a man, but as is true for the nipples, this area is almost too sensitive to touch.
- *Gentle massage* of the man's chest, back, stomach and hips gives him pleasure. Body massage produces a slow, sensual form of excitement. The man can enjoy it and yet keep his rising excitement under control.
- *Letting the fingers play* lightly over the penis, scrotum and anus gives pleasure without causing too much excitement. Light touch is preferable to firm or vigorous manipulation, at least in the early stages of lovemaking. From a man's standpoint, the most enjoyable way for a wife to stimulate the penis is with her mouth or tongue. Many couples find this an exciting prelude to sexual intercourse.

The sensitivity of a man's skin goes up as his excitement increases. He may reach the point, in fact, of not being able to stand much stroking or fondling of his body. In time, a wife will learn how to stimulate her husband slowly and pleasurably. The idea is for the couple to climb together toward the height of ecstasy— orgasm.

Orgasm

The most enjoyable part of a man's role in sexual love comes at the moment of orgasm. The feeling is like no other. It's delicious and satisfying and fulfilling, and with it comes a sweet sense of relief and relaxation. The man ejaculates, and the sperm cells in his semen are what make it possible for his wife to become pregnant.

Semen: A Man's Product

The semen is a teaspoonful of sticky liquid that is clear to milky in color. It contains hundreds of millions of sperm cells, though only one sperm actually fertilizes the egg to produce a pregnancy. The semen has many origins:

● *The testicles make the sperm cells.* Each testicle is a soft, spongy-feeling organ about an inch wide and an inch and a half long. A man has two testicles. One hangs lower than the other, and this prevents them from being pressed together and injured.

● *The vas deferens* is the tube that carries sperm cells from the testicles toward the opening in the back part of the penis. Each testicle has a vas deferens, and the tube serves as a storage place for sperm cells.

● *The seminal vesicles* lie on either side of the man's bladder near where the vas deferens enters the penis. They contribute to the fluid content of semen.

● *The prostate gland* supplies most of the volume of the semen. It is a plum-sized gland that sits just below the man's bladder and at the back part of the penis. It and the seminal vesicles can produce semen very rapidly, but only within certain limits. When a man has several orgasms in one day, the volume of semen produced at each ejaculation goes down. By the same token, if he's gone several weeks without an orgasm he will have saved up a lot of fluid for release the next time he makes love.

A small amount of fluid may come out of the erect penis before the man ejaculates. This clear fluid is sometimes called "glad come" or preejaculation fluid. It is made in the Cowper's glands, two pea-sized glands that sit high up in the base of the penis. The purpose of this thin discharge is to lubricate the inside of the penis to make it easier for semen to be squirted out. Sperm cells get into the Cowper's gland fluid of about 25% of men, and thus a wife could become pregnant even when her husband doesn't ejaculate.

The Special Thing about a Man's Orgasm

The special thing about a man's orgasm is that the longer he goes without one, the more enjoyable it becomes when he has it. Within certain limits, nature seems to encourage a man to save up his semen. A man who experiences several orgasms in one day discovers that each is a little less pleasurable than the one before.

A woman is different. She is physically capable of having one orgasm after another, each more exciting than the one before. A man can't do this. He builds to one giant pitch of excitement, ejaculates, and then must wait for a while before having intercourse again. After orgasm his excitement goes down and within several minutes he loses his erection. The time it will take him to regain it varies from one man to another. It may take only 10 or 15 minutes, or a day or a week. In general, the younger the man the stronger his sex drive, and the more quickly he'll be able to have another erection. To repeat, the quality of sexual love is more important than its frequency. A man's role is to express his love for his wife in the most intimate and pleasurable way possible. Lovemaking leads to ejaculation and the spilling of his seed, and allows the couple to create a new life if they wish.

The wife is an equal partner in the sexual relationship. In the next chapter we'll discuss her role in sexual love.

4

The Woman's Role
in Sexual Love

One of the truly remarkable developments of the last few years has been the awakening of interest in a woman's sexuality. Gone forever is the notion that many women are "frigid," or that a wife must take a passive role in sexual love. A woman is an equal partner in lovemaking, and in fact, she can enjoy sex more than her husband. For one thing, she is capable of having multiple orgasms—a feat that her husband cannot duplicate. Still another thing in a woman's favor is that her interest in sex tends to increase during her thirties, forties, and fifties. Thus, by taking an active role in lovemaking she stands to increase her own pleasure and that of her husband.

A woman's anatomy, sexuality and responsiveness to lovemaking are the subject of this chapter.

The Unique Features of a Woman's Anatomy

A woman's skin is soft, her breasts are prominent, her hips are full. Two sex hormones, *estrogen* and *progesterone*, produce these distinctly feminine changes.

Magic Chemicals

At the age of puberty, a woman begins to have menstrual periods. The periods will continue until she is 45 or 50 years old. Each month, one of her ovaries will release an egg. That ovary also produces estrogen and progesterone, and the sex hormones enter the woman's bloodstream. The hormones serve two purposes. They enable her to get pregnant, and they bring on the body changes that transform a girl into a woman.

To make pregnancy possible, the two chemicals cause the womb to store nutrients that will feed the egg during the first few days and weeks after it is fertilized by the husband's sperm. If the woman doesn't become pregnant, her womb sheds its inner lining at the time of the menstrual bleeding. Ordinarily, a woman has a menstrual period about once a month, and the bleeding lasts 3-6 days.

"Mad Desire"

Estrogen and progesterone also soften a woman's skin, cause her hips and breasts to enlarge, and give her the graceful appearance of a mature woman. Indeed, the word *estrogen* means "to produce mad desire." The "mad desire" refers to the effects a blossoming young woman's body may have on a man. The woman owes her feminine softness to a layer of fat under her skin. The fat makes her more desirable to the opposite sex, and serves as a food reservoir she can use during pregnancy. Her sex hormones cause a woman to have less body hair than a man, though hair still grows around her genitals, under her arms, and on her legs. Perhaps the most specific changes produced by estrogen occur in the woman's vulva, vagina, and clitoris.

The Vulva

"Vulva" means covering. It refers to the outside parts of a woman's genitals, and includes the pubic hair and the pad of skin beneath it, as well as the skin folds that cover the entrance to the vagina.

• *The pubic hair* tends to grow in the shape of a triangle with a horizontal upper border. (However, a normal woman's pubic hair may tent upwards toward her belly button just like a man's.) Her pubic hair is one of a woman's sexiest parts. By caressing it, a husband can give his wife pleasure—and the mere sight of it may give him pleasure. A wife may get the idea that she'd be sexier without this hair. Not so! One couple came in for marital counseling, and the wife turned out to be

The Woman Who Shaved in the Wrong Place

Ronald and Kathy had four children, and had enjoyed a good sexual relationship. One day Kathy decided to try something she'd read in a book. She shaved off her pubic hair. That night she surprised Ronald, and he was flabbergasted! He made love to her, but then seemed to lose interest in sex. Not understanding the reason, Kathy became frustrated. Ronald could have saved her a lot of worry by coming right out and telling her that he preferred her the natural way. He finally did admit this, but not until I'd suggested that it was the best way to solve the problem. Ronald and Kathy began to enjoy a happy sex life again when she let her hair grow back.

• *The mons* (rhymes with "ponds") is the soft pad of skin just beneath a woman's pubic hair. It enjoys a rich nerve supply, and is a sensitive part of the female genital organs. Another name for it is the *mons veneris*, or mount of Venus—named for the goddess of love.

• *The main lips* are the soft folds of skin just below the mons. These lips meet in the midline to cover the entrance to the vagina. They, too, are richly supplied with nerves, and are sensitive to the husband's touch during foreplay.

• *The minor lips*, much thinner than the main lips, are delicate folds of skin just inside the main lips. Their size varies, but they enlarge during sexual excitement.

The Vagina

The vagina is the woman's sex organ. In shape, size and design, it is ideally suited to receive the man's penis. At puberty, a woman's sex hormones cause the cells in the vagina to thicken and multiply. The vagina enlarges, but the size of a mature woman's vagina depends on many things. The organ gets bigger after she's begun to have sexual relations, and it becomes roomier after she's had children. On the other hand, repair of the cut made at childbirth will keep the vaginal opening almost as snug as if the woman hadn't had children.

Think of the vagina as a pouch or pocket. Its walls and boundaries are definite, but when it isn't in use it folds in on itself. The bladder may push down on it from above, and the rectum may push up on it from below. The pouch will get bigger to accommodate the husband's penis during lovemaking, and muscles around the vagina will provide just the right amount of inward pressure. (How a woman can use these muscles to increase her sexual pleasure is discussed in Chapter 11.)

The average length of the vagina in women who haven't had children is a little over three inches. The average width is an inch and a half. A woman's sexual excitement causes her vagina to get bigger. It can enlarge to a length of four and a half inches and a width at its blind end of almost three inches. Early in marriage, a couple must be aware that the vagina enlarges most when the wife is strongly aroused. One couple had a problem because of

The Husband Who Tried to Do Too Much Too Soon

Ed and Monica were newlyweds. Monica wanted very much to have pleasurable sex with her husband, but couldn't. The pain she experienced when Ed entered her overcame her feelings of arousal and made the act one of total discomfort. An examination showed that Monica's vagina was below average in size. Even so, it would dilate to an adequate size when she was sexually aroused.

Ed hadn't been taking the time to make sure that his wife was strongly aroused. He was very excitable himself, and presumed that Monica was the same. Once he understood the differences between a man's and a woman's rates of arousal, he proceeded more slowly. Ed's slow and sensual lovemaking technique gave Monica the time she needed to become fully aroused and ready for intercourse. She began to enjoy sex, and Ed was pleased by the intercourse and by his ability to please his wife.

The Clitoris

The clitoris is a small and sensitive structure that sits well above the vagina inside folds of the minor lips. It is protected by the main lips and mons. It isn't big enough to be easily seen unless you specifically look for it, but it can be felt as a tubular structure about an inch long and as big around as a kitchen match.

The sole purpose of the clitoris is to increase a woman's enjoyment of sex. Its position lets it be stimulated by any movement of the vulva or vagina during sexual excitement, and its role in lovemaking will be discussed below.

Sexual Excitement in a Woman

Women are just as sexually excitable as men—maybe more so. Dr. Alfred Kinsey found that 2% of women could reach a sexual climax just by thinking sexy thoughts. It's almost impossible for a man to do this. Sexy thoughts may play a role in a wife's arousal, but stimulation of her body is usually necessary for her to reach the plateau of excitement that leads to enjoyable sexual intercourse.

A Woman's Erogenous Zones

Every part of a wife's body is sensitive to her husband's touch. One woman I knew of could become sexually excited by having her husband rub his fingers through her hair. Another told me that the lightest touch of her husband's fingers on the tips of her own was enough to send her into ecstasy! Most women readily admit that some parts of their body are more sensitive than others. In approximate order of sensitivity, here are a woman's erogenous zones:

- *The clitoris*
- *The minor lips of the vulva*
- *The mons and main lips*
- *The breasts and nipples*
- *Mouth and ears*
- *Palms and fingertips*

- *Armpits*
- *Thighs*
- *Lower belly*
- *Chest*
- *Back and hips*
- *Legs*

One part of the Sensual Union training—discussed in the next two chapters—is for the husband to explore his wife's body and find out what gives her the most pleasure. A common mistake is to presume that since the clitoris is the most sensitive part of a woman's anatomy, stimulation of it comes first. Most women prefer stimulation of other body parts in the early phases of sexual excitement. Consider the case of

The Man Who Made the Mistake of the "Experts"

Duane D. was married for a second time, and was disappointed with his sex life. At first he and his wife had enjoyed sexual relations, but Duane had begun to read marriage manuals in the hope of increasing their enjoyment. Book after book talked about the wife's clitoris, and how it had to be stimulated for her to reach an orgasm. He applied what he read to Sue, his wife, but she reacted differently to what he'd expected. Sue said that Duane's manipulation of her clitoris was painful. Duane couldn't believe the "experts" were wrong, and persisted in trying to turn his wife on by stimulating her clitoris. Sue began to refuse his attempts to have sex with her, and Duane came into the office for a discussion of the problem.

I pointed out that the information given in some marriage

manuals is misleading. The clitoris is important to a wife's enjoyment of sex, but a husband needs to remember three things:

1. *Stimulation of the clitoris* early in foreplay tends to cause pain rather than pleasure.
2. *Direct stimulation* of the clitoris is not necessary for a woman to have an orgasm.
3. *Women who enjoy clitoral stimulation* usually prefer light stroking or caressing of the skin just above or near the clitoris.

"By all means read about sex," I told Duane, "but let your wife be your guide. No two people are alike. Your goal in sexual relations is mutual pleasure. If something gives you that, do it. If it causes pain, avoid it."

I would give the same advice to any couple!

The Role of the Clitoris in Lovemaking

The clitoris is located above the vagina and tucked into skin folds for a reason. It's too sensitive to be right out in the open. Early in a woman's sexual excitement, the end of her clitoris will enlarge slightly. Its enlargement lets the clitoris sit more snugly within its hood of skin. Thus, any movement of the mons, the main lips or the minor lips will indirectly stimulate it. Indeed, most women who masturbate do so by stimulating the skin above and around the clitoris rather than directly touching the organ. Masters and Johnson found this to be true in their studies, and Shere Hite confirmed it in *The Hite Report*, her book describing a nationwide study of the sexual attitudes and practices of 3,000 women aged 14-78.

As a woman's sexual excitement carries her into the plateau phase of sexual intercourse, her clitoris withdraws into the skin folds of the minor lips. This protects it from the thrusting of the husband's penis during intercourse. However, movement of the penis in the vagina does continue to stimulate the clitoris. The vagina is a pocket, remember, and as the penis pushes against the walls of the pocket the motion is transmitted through the lips of the vulva to the clitoris. This means that when the couple are having relations in the man-on-top position, the husband doesn't have to "ride high" by forcing the base of his penis against the clitoris. If the couple enjoys this, fine, but the clitoris will be stimulated by sexual intercourse in any position. As was mentioned in Chapter 2, the woman on top position is the best for clitoral stimulation.

In summary, the clitoris is the most sensitive part of the woman's genitals. Direct stimulation of it early in a woman's sexual excitement may cause pain rather than pleasure. The clitoris is stimulated during sexual intercourse, and this stimulation contributes to a woman's excitement and eventual orgasm. Wise is the husband who will focus the early parts of his lovemaking not on the wife's clitoris or vulva, but on the other parts of her body.

The Sex Flush

Sexual excitement stimulates every part of a woman's body. Arousal causes her heart rate and breathing rate to go up; her body temperature may rise. About three-fourths of women develop a measles-like skin rash when sexually excited. The skin rash is called the sex flush.

It appears on the woman's stomach and chest late in the excitement or early in the plateau phase of sexual response. The rash spreads to her breasts, lower tummy, and shoulders. As she nears her sexual climax, a woman may have the rash on her back, thighs and buttocks. The greater the woman's excitement, the more extensive will be her sex flush.

Things a Man Can Do to Excite His Wife

A woman's sexual excitement differs in two ways from a man's. First, it occurs more slowly, and second, it is more dependent on body stimulation. The husband who would be a good lover has to go slowly, and he has to develop a feeling for stimulating the right part of his wife's body in the right way at the right time.

One cannot make a definite statement about what is right for every couple, but discovering what turns the mate on is one of the fun things about lovemaking. Here are some of the reactions a husband might expect from fondling his wife's body:

- *Lightly touching* her fingers and palms will give the wife a tingly feeling of excitement. The skin on the inside of a woman's arms is very sensitive, and becomes more so as the stroking draws nearer the breast.
- *Gentle massage* of her back, buttocks and thighs will give pleasure to a woman. Body massage is a luxurious and pleasurable form of stimulation.
- *Kissing* is very exciting to most women. It's exciting to a man, too, but some husbands tend to forget about it after marriage. They shouldn't. The tongue is a most artful organ, and you can say a lot with it without uttering a word.
- *Caressing a woman's ears* and eyes with the lips and fingers is a way of exciting her. Light caressing and gentle kissing are preferable early in foreplay.
- *Gentle fondling* of the wife's breasts can excite her and her husband. The nipple is the most sensitive part of the breast, so the caressing should begin at the outer edge of the breast and gradually work inward. A woman's breasts enlarge during sexual excitement. Her nipples harden and become more prominent. Tweaking, kissing or fondling the nipples will give the woman pleasure.
- *Touching her thighs and vulva* can add to the pleasure of a wife already excited by stimulation of other body parts. At first, the touching should be light and brief, and interposed with other forms of stimulation. Later the exploration of the vulva can be intimate and thorough.

Changes in the Main and Minor Lips

The main lips of her vulva are quite prominent when a woman isn't sexually excited. As her sexual tension rises, these lips tend to flatten out and become less noticeable. This has the effect of making the vagina more accessible to the husband's penis.

The main lips get smaller, but the minor lips get bigger. The delicate folds of skin surround the vaginal opening, and their enlargement has the effect of lengthening the vagina. The lips also change color when the woman becomes aroused. The minor lips of a woman who's never had children turn a pink or bright red color during sexual excitement, while the color change is to bright red or a deep wine color if the woman has had children.

How the Vagina Prepares for Intercourse

Sexual excitement causes the vagina to enlarge, and its walls begin to release a natural oil to serve as a lubricant for intercourse.

The rule about the size of a woman's vagina is that any vagina will accommodate any penis, so long as the wife is aroused sufficiently before her husband attempts to enter her. Gentleness, understanding and love will allow the couple to have enjoyable intercourse. The new wife will find that she has less discomfort during intercourse (if it occurs at all) as she and her husband become sexually adjusted to one another.

The vagina is squishy wet even when a woman isn't excited. Very soon after the onset of her arousal, however, she begins to produce a natural lubricant. It wells out in sweat-like droplets from all parts of the vagina, and may even seep out of the organ to appear on the vulva. Thin and light, the oil is slippery enough to let the penis slide easily into the vagina. Masters and Johnson found that a woman begins to release this oil only 10-30 seconds after the onset of her sexual excitement. Theoretically, she's ready for intercourse. Actually, she may not be. A woman will enjoy sex much more if her husband waits until her entire body is responsive to him. Many couples have told me that the longer they spend arousing one another, the more they enjoy the moment of insertion.

A Woman's Orgasm

A woman's orgasm, or sexual climax, is a supremely pleasurable event. It brings a release of tension and a feeling of joy and satisfaction. Her vaginal oils may flow out of the vagina and make it appear as though she's ejaculated. A woman doesn't produce "come" in the same sense as a man, but her orgasm does resemble his in other ways.

The Feeling Itself

The experience is like no other. It's a moment of ecstasy, a feeling of rapture beyond comparison. Her heart may have been beating rapidly during sexual excitement, but at the moment of orgasm it will be racing at twice its normal rate. Covered with a sex flush, the woman may perspire, breathe heavily and grimace. The muscles throughout her body go into rhythmic spasms. It can be an overwhelming experience, and leave the woman feeling exhausted and happy.

The pleasurable sensations begin in the clitoris and vagina, then spread throughout the body. Masters and Johnson found that a woman's orgasm consists of several components. First the woman feels that everything in the world has come to a screeching halt. Then she becomes aware of a deep feeling of pleasure and warmth in her vagina and pelvic region. The feeling flows from her pelvis into the rest of her body. Finally, the woman becomes aware of a throbbing throughout her body. The orgasm lasts for several seconds, and subsides slowly.

Multiple Orgasms

Something many husbands don't realize is that a woman is capable of having multiple orgasms, one right after another. The interval between orgasms may vary from a few seconds to a few minutes. Some women find that each subsequent orgasm is better than the one before, while others claim that one is enough and two is too many. A person who reported her experience in *The Hite Report* had this to say: "One orgasm is always sexually satisfying for me. I don't know how many I'm capable of because I never want to go beyond just one. I think I reach such a high, such a state of ecstasy that to go beyond it would take away from that peak. It takes a while for my body to feel normal afterwards anyway.''[1]

Of course, no two women are alike. Nor is a wife going to approach sex in exactly the same way two nights in a row. Her needs and wishes may differ from one time to the next. The important thing for the husband to remember is that his wife is capable of great heights of ecstasy. By controlling his own pitch of excitement, he can let her have more than one climax. Then again, the wife shouldn't feel that she has to achieve an orgasm to enjoy sex. Many of the women in *The Hite Report* said that they enjoyed sexual arousal more than the actual moment of climax. One woman felt that orgasm was a disappointment because it meant the end of sexual arousal. What it boils down to is that each couple must develop lovemaking techniques that are right for them.

A Woman's Sexuality

Lovemaking is focused on the genitals, but a woman's most important sex organ is her brain. A clean, open feeling about sex will let her get the maximum amount of pleasure from marital relations.

Influence of Past Attitudes

A woman's sexual character consists of many different parts. She is the sum of everything that she has seen, heard and felt. However, some influences are stronger than others. A girl who is taught from an early age that sex is dirty or nasty may have difficulty shedding this notion after marriage. I'm reminded of

---

[1]Shere Hite, *The Hite Report*, Macmillan, New York, 1976, p. 90.

The Woman Who Began Enjoying Sex
When She Knew That She Could

Sherry and Robert had been married for less than a year, but were headed for divorce. At the suggestion of friends, they sought counseling. Sherry was reluctant to talk about their sexual problem, but Robert wasn't. "My wife wouldn't let me touch her the night we were married," he said bitterly. "I was gentle and wanted to love her, but she just kept saying she didn't want to, that we would later. Well, 'later' turned out to be *three weeks* later. And then she cried afterward and that made me feel terrible. We've made love several times since then, but our marriage is just not working the way it should. Frankly, I'm disappointed. I love Sherry, but our sex is not what it should be."

Sherry didn't wish to speak in front of her husband, but when we were alone she told me the source of her problem: her mother. She'd been raised in a strictly religious home, and her mother had spent hours and hours telling her about the sins of sex and the terrible disgrace it would be if she became pregnant before she was married. By the time she was old enough to date, Sherry felt guilty just sitting close to a boy, much less kissing him. She'd hoped that marriage would change her feelings, but it didn't. What caused most of the guilt, though, was that Sherry liked sex with her husband. She was convinced that anything that felt that good had to be wrong.

I assured her that sexual relations between husband and wife were perfectly natural and not wrong in any way. With her own efforts and the help of her husband, Sherry was able to work through her guilt feelings and accept sex as a normal part of married life. Within a few weeks, she and Robert began to enjoy an active and pleasurable sex life.

Learning to Do What Comes Naturally

Sherry's problem was unusually severe, but it's not that rare for a woman to have negative feelings about sex. She may have grown up hearing stories about unwed mothers, venereal disease or "nice girls" and "bad girls." After marriage, her doubts about sex may remain. Some signs of an uncertain attitude about sex are when a wife:

- *Feels guilty about having sexual intercourse with her husband.*
- *Won't remove all her clothing before sexual intercourse.*
- *Is unwilling to have sex except in total darkness.*
- *Avoids looking at her own nude body or that of her husband.*
- *Feels that she must "warn" her children about the dangers of sex.*

A woman who has these feelings may still enjoy sex, but she'll enjoy it more if she accepts it as the natural, pleasurable part of life that it is. The body is to be appreciated and loved. Who can appreciate it more than a marriage partner, and what could be more loving than sharing physical pleasure?

A Note on Sexual Equality

More and more women are not only taking a healthy, open view of sex, they're demanding sexual equality. This has its good and its bad parts. In the first place, the wife is and should be an equal partner in lovemaking. She needn't take a passive role in sexual relations, and this means that she's free to initiate sex or set the pace of lovemaking. The bad part is that some husbands just aren't ready to accept the wife's equality. I'll use as an example

The Man Who Felt Threatened
by His Wife

Wanda and Steve were a young couple who enjoyed sex. Steve was an outgoing, aggressive individual who was already a vice president in his company. One night after work he was sitting on the edge of the bed watching TV. He looked up to see Wanda standing in front of him. She had removed her clothing and was wearing a very inviting smile. It was the first time in three years of marriage that Wanda had tried to initiate sex. Earlier in the day she'd been reading a sexy book, and had decided to appear in the nude in front of her husband to see what would happen. What happened was not what she'd expected.

Steve quickly removed his clothing and embraced his wife, but he couldn't get an erection. It was the first time he had failed to do so, and he fretted and worried about it. Later that evening he initiated sex and performed quite well.

Steve told me what had happened, and it was apparent that he perceived his wife's provocative behavior as a threat to his manhood. He saw himself as the leader, the sexual aggressor. His wife taking that role shocked him. I suggested that he might enjoy a little variation, that many husbands found role reversal to be an exciting variation in lovemaking. He smiled and agreed. He'd thought about what Wanda had done, and liked it. "It was just that the first time was such a surprise. But I think I can handle it now."

An Active Wife Means a Happy Husband

Steve and Wanda could have avoided their temporary difficulty if somewhere along the way they'd discussed her taking the initiative. This is an area for love, understanding, and cooperation. Actually, the husband has everything to gain from accepting his wife's sexual equality.

Dr. William Masters has pointed out that a man may come to feel that his sexual role is stereotyped. His having to be the aggressor may deprive him of some of the pleasure of sex: "In the long run, the trend toward sexual equality should mean a great deal for both male and female. As she assumes a share of the responsibility for making something happen between them, her self-esteem should rise, and with that should come an intensified capacity for pleasure. And as the male is relieved of some of the pressure his pleasure too should be increased—and, within limits, his performance as well!''[2] Marabel Morgan made her point about equality when she advised the wife to never let her hands be still during intercourse.[3]

A Loving Wife's Most Precious Gift

At its best, the sexual love between a wife and her husband should get better with the passage of time. The woman's role is to give and receive pleasure—simple as that! She is the only one who can decide what is enjoyable for her, and what brings pleasure to her is what she should do. Her most precious gift to her husband, in fact, is her love. If she loves him more than anything in the world, and shows that love, they'll have good sex.

What is right for one couple may be wrong for another, but one thing holds true for all marriages. The goal of sex is mutual pleasure. Sexual happiness is something a husband and wife can find and enjoy together. In the following two chapters we'll continue discussing how to get more pleasure out of sex.

---

[2] William H. Masters and Virginia E. Johnson (with Robert J. Levin), *The Pleasure Bond*, Little, Brown and Co., Boston, 1970, pp. 73-74.

[3] Marabel Morgan, *op. cit.*

5

The Sensual Union
—Week One

*T*he husband and wife who get the most from the sexual side of marriage have what I choose to call a Sensual Union. They are happy, and their marriage remains new and exciting and pleasurable. In many ways, they're like teen-agers in love. They may have been married for 20 or 30 years or more, but they still share things, still flirt with one another, still get a kick out of being together. In bed, they find happiness in natural, uninhibited sex, because each has learned the joy of giving and of receiving pleasure. The main thing is that their marriage is fun. The purpose of this chapter and the following chapter is to give the eight steps showing how every couple can enjoy a Sensual Union.

What the Sensual Union Does

Sex was meant to be fun! Nature made it that way to ensure the very necessary act of reproduction. Sensual Union training emphasizes the pleasurable things that a husband and wife can do together. Of course, some couples learn these techniques on their own, and continue to apply them throughout their years of marriage.

Other couples may need some help. The training discussed here can serve as a refresher course for the sexually happy couple, or it can show how a man and wife who've noticed less interest in sex can reawaken their desire for one another.

Dr. William Masters and Dr. Virginia Johnson of The Reproductive Biology Research Foundation, St. Louis, Missouri have led the way in showing how married couples can bring freshness and excitement into their lovemaking, and I'm indebted to them and to other researchers for some of the techniques that are described in the Sensual Union. However, the information in these two chapters comes from many different sources. I've selected what I feel are the best ways for a couple to get more joy out of sex.

Two Weeks to a Happier Marriage

The program is meant to help you and your mate achieve a Sensual Union in just two weeks. Of course, each couple will tend to go at their own rate. A little something new introduced into the sexual relationship may pep up your marriage in only one night. Or, you may need several months of mutual effort to reach the full joy of a Sensual Union. Two weeks is about the average length of time, but the Sensual Union is not something that ends after two weeks. It is an ongoing relationship, and there's no upper limit to how long you and your mate can spend developing it. After you know the basic techniques, you can spend the rest of your lives improving on them. The steps in this chapter are to be taken up during the first week, and the program for the second week appears in the next chapter.

The Sensual Union: The Program for Week One

The goal of Sensual Union training is to introduce you and your mate to the ways you can get more pleasure out of lovemaking. The program is meant to be done a step at a time, but it's perfectly all right to read the entire program before beginning it. However, it's best to take up the instructions in the same order that they are given. The first week of the program consists of these four steps:

STEP ONE: *Put Some Fun into Sex.*
STEP TWO: *Benefit from the Joys of a Sensuous Massage.*
STEP THREE: *Explore Your Mate's Body for New Ways to Build Sexual Excitement.*
STEP FOUR: *Begin to Try New Things Together.*

Step One: Put Some Fun into Sex.

Sex can be fun, but not unless you and your mate are relaxed and willing to have a good time in bed! Too many people have the mistaken idea that sex is a performance. They expect to achieve a certain goal, and are disappointed when they don't. The first step to making sex fun is to relieve yourself of any pressure you may feel to perform in a certain way. Talk this over with your mate. Level with each other. Agree that starting now, THE GOAL OF YOUR SEX LIFE WILL BE TO HAVE FUN. That's all. The Sensual Union is a pleasurable one, and here are three ways to make sex fun:

Three Ways to Make Sex Fun

1. *Get sexy with your partner!*
2. *Explore new techniques of sexual arousal.*
3. *Become an expert lover!*

1. Get Sexy with Your Partner!

Getting sexy with your marital partner means just that. Take a new interest in each other's sexual likes and dislikes. Do what your mate likes, and avoid what he or she doesn't like. One woman who was having difficulty letting herself go was offended because her husband used "dirty" words during their lovemaking. She found these words offensive—until I pointed out that during intimacies between husband and wife no words that intensify sensual feelings need be considered bad. The woman stopped taking offense, and to her surprise found that using a "forbidden" word or two gave her a measure of sexual release that she hadn't expected. Another woman took it a step further.

How Ellie Learned to Ring
Her Husband's Bell

Ellie and Bill had been married for fifteen years, but their sex life had long since lost its zip. One day Ellie and a friend were comparing notes, and the subject got around to sex. Ellie's friend claimed that she had discovered a secret way of turning a man on. "I become the aggressor," she said. "I put my mouth and tongue to his ear and whisper sexy things about his body and about how I crave him. I'm telling you, he loves it."

Ellie decided to try this technique on her husband. She called his office that afternoon, but when she heard his familiar voice say hello, she just couldn't say what she'd intended to say. Instead, she asked him when he was going to get home, and if he had any preferences for supper.

That night after dinner, Bill mentioned the phone call. "Gee, it was good to hear your voice," he said. "It perked up the rest of the afternoon and made me start thinking about what I had waiting for me here at home. You know, you sound very sexy on the phone." Bill kissed his wife and led her into the bedroom. Their sex was better than it had been in months.

Encouraged, Ellie decided to try the phone idea again. She did, and soon she was able to whisper all the sexy things she'd wanted to say to her husband the first time she called. Not all of her calls were long ones. She might just say, "I'm crazy about your body," and hang up, or tell him that she had a yearning for him in one certain spot that only he could fill. Before Ellie began to call Bill, he sometimes lingered late at the office or stopped off for a drink on the way home. After she began getting sexy with him, Bill came straight home. He liked to let out a whoop, swoop her into his arms, and hug her and kiss her as if he hadn't seen her in weeks. Ellie's bold initiative had rejuvenated their sex life.

Getting sexy with your marriage partner can take many forms. A hug when you first see one another at the end of the day can be a sensual experience. So can a bright, cheery smile. Buying his wife lingerie is a tried and proven way for a husband to be sexy. One man I knew left suggestive notes for his wife to find during the day. One afternoon the wife was looking through her dresser and found a skimpy pair of see-through bikini panties that her husband had given her some months before. Pinned to them was a note saying: "Wear these and nothing else tonight at supper. Love ya!" She complied. Were they a sensual couple? Of course! They'd learned that it is the sexy little things a husband and wife do for each other that make the sexy big thing (intercourse) more fun.

2. Explore New Techniques of Sexual Arousal.

You can arouse your mate in many ways, but do you? A key part of the Sensual Union is to find new and exciting forms of sexual stimulation. The same old lovemaking techniques can get boring, if for no other reason than that your partner knows what to expect. Change! Do things differently.

How Charlie Turned His Wife On

Charlie and Louise had been married for ten years, and rated their sex life as "average." One day he read in a magazine that the man wasn't the only one who could be turned on by seeing the partner's body. So could a woman. Charlie was a weight lifter, but he always confined his workouts to the gym. On a hunch, he wore his weight-lifting trunks home beneath his clothing that evening. He undressed to reveal his hairy, muscular body and the very tight gym shorts. Louise stood like a weak-kneed cheerleader as her husband pumped up his big muscles by lifting chairs in the kitchen, by doing handstands, and by tilting the sofa over with one finger. At the height of his performance, he swooped his wife into his arms and carried her into the bedroom where he made passionate love to her. Charlie was as surprised at Louise as she was at him. He had never imagined that she could be so responsive!

Sex during the day can be an exciting event for a man. His wife is more visible, and he may derive a lot of pleasure from seeing her body. He may enjoy undressing her in front of a mirror, or having her stand so that she can watch her reaction to him kissing her breasts and stimulating the other parts of her body. Men notice a woman's undergarments, and the wife can appear more seductive by dressing in different kinds of lingerie and letting her husband see it. The man may prefer that his wife leave her pants and bra on until the start of sex play, because removing these items can be sexually stimulating. By the same token, the wife may prefer that her husband leave his clothes on so that she can have the fun of removing them. One thing most men are wild about is the sight of a woman wearing hose and garter belt, but little else.

How Sue Ella Put Some Fire into Her Marriage

Sue Ella and Richard were just home from church early on a Sunday afternoon. They were alone in the bedroom planning a picnic and changing clothes. Sue Ella noticed that her husband was watching her. "Those hose," he said, "and the way your legs look in them! I never noticed how sexy you are! Come here to me." Sue Ella started to remove the hose, but her husband stopped her. He drew down her panties and made love to her on the floor of their walk-in closet. The two emerged from the bedroom half an hour later, smiling. The family had their picnic, and Richard made love to his wife again that evening. He hadn't shown so much interest in sex in years, and Sue Ella asked him what had caused it.

"I think seeing you in those hose is what did it," he said. "That sexed me up, and so did seeing those lines the panties left on your skin, and the way your hair was all matted down. I guess I didn't realize how lucky I am to have such a sexy, good-looking woman for my wife."

Sue Ella was highly pleased by her husband's reaction to her. Accidentally she had learned to put some fire into her marriage by showing her husband a different view of her than he usually saw. Making love while wearing hose and garter belt wasn't something that she would do every time, but it was a fresh and exciting thing for Richard. It was a new arousal technique.

Husband and wife can both wear sexy underthings. The garments are available in most clothing stores. A wife can start by wearing bikini panties or the slightly larger ones known as "hip huggers." Years ago I went to the store to buy my wife some lingerie, and was waited on by a middle-aged woman. She blushed when I asked to see the bikini panties, and I could tell she wanted to say something. As I was paying for the purchase she said, "You know, until a few months ago I thought it was a sin to wear bikini underwear. But one of my friends told me she did, and that I ought to try them. She's a good Christian woman, and I took her advice. And you know what? They're comfortable! I've thrown away my others, and this is the only kind I wear now. Isn't it silly what notions we get about things?"

Of course it's silly if the notion keeps you from wearing what you want to wear or what will give you and your mate sensual pleasure! By all means wear sexy underwear if you want to do so! Your fancy may even run to the slightly more erotic items available in novelty shops or through the mail from Adam & Eve or similar companies.

3. Become an Expert Lover!

How do you become an expert lover? By using your brain and your body. Your brain is nothing if not a love organ, so take advantage of it! Notice your mate's responses to lovemaking; find what is successful and do more of it. After all, you get to see your partner's body and how it responds to lovemaking. What better person to become an expert on a wife's body than her husband? Or on a husband's body than his wife?

The brain and the body work together, of course, but in the Sensual Union they work in concert. A husband might enjoy having his face rubbed by his wife's breasts; she might like for him to kiss her all over in places that will thrill her and maybe even embarrass her a little. A good way to become an expert lover is to take up the ancient and sexy practice of sensual massage. The massage itself can be an erotic and pleasurable experience, and it can be the starting point for an intimate exploration of the partner's body.

Step Two: Benefit from the Joys of a Sensuous Massage.

Your fingers and hands are marvelous and sensitive sex organs! Use them to titillate, arouse and give pleasure to your mate's body. An irresistible way to do this is by giving him or her a rubdown using a light, slippery body oil. The massage is fun, and it feels good. When you've finished with your mate, it's your turn. The massages may be a prelude to sexual intercourse, may lead up to the explorations discussed in Step Three, or may be pleasurable in and of themselves without the need for progressing to further sex play. The sensuous massage is a basic technique of the Sensual Union, and discovering the many subtleties of it is fun. Here are some tips on how to get the most out of this very sensual experience.

How to Get the Most
Out of a Very Sensual Experience

1. Begin the sensuous massages on the first day of the Sensual Union program. It doesn't matter whether you or your mate goes first; just take turns and give one another the massages every day for the first week of training. Continue to make the massages a part of your lovemaking at least once a week.

2. *Prepare for the massages* by removing your own clothing or undressing one another. Complete disrobing to allow total nudity adds to the sensuality of the experience. It's a good idea to spread a couple of sheets or towels on top of the bed to catch any oil that may spill during the massage. Finally, set the mood. If you drink, you may enjoy some wine or liqueur before beginning. Background music is a must. The music can be country western, popular, exotic or Oriental. I know of a couple who play Beethoven and other classical records during their lovemaking; still another couple prefer the jouncy rhythms of John Philip Sousa band music. If you have no preference, try soft music such as that played by many FM stations. Finally, turn the lights down but not out.

3. *Choose an oil that is light and slippery.* Kama Sutra Oil of Love is a product made for giving sensual massages, but many similar products are on the market. You can find perfectly adequate oils at the drugstore. Among these are Alpha-Keri®, Nivea®, Lubath®, and Demol®. Alpha-Keri is the one I recommend—the *bath oil*, not the skin lotion. (The skin oil can be used, but tends to be a little too heavy for easy massage.) Alpha-Keri bath oil is a turquoise-colored product that comes in 4, 8 and 16-ounce bottles. If your druggist is nosy, explain the purchase by saying that you have dry skin. The oil is good for dry skin, but it's even better for a sensuous massage. An eight-ounce bottle should provide enough oil for a dozen massages.

The Way Mary W. Turned Her Man On

Mary's husband, Bob, worked in the construction industry as a foreman. His job called for long hours and hard work, and many times he was so tired at the end of the day that he fell asleep on the sofa. Mary found out about the sensual massage, and when she mentioned giving him one, her husband moaned pleasurably. He showered, and Mary rubbed him down with olive oil from her kitchen (it's another excellent oil for this purpose). Bob was so turned on by the experience that he insisted on returning the favor, and the intimacies led into the best sex they'd had in years. Bob told Mary that one of his favorite fantasies was of being rubbed down like that, but that asking his wife to do it was something that had never occurred to him. Now the two of them enjoy this delicious experience often.

4. *Use light, circular hand and finger motions* during the massage. Go ahead and knead the mate's shoulders, neck and back if it feels good, but apply light, gentle stroking to the rest of the body. The secret of a tingling massage is to start in an insensitive area and work teasingly toward a more sensitive one. Begin with your mate lying face down. Pour oil into your palm, and apply it to the middle of the back. Use your fingers and palms to spread the oil in ever-widening circles over the shoulders and neck, the hips and thighs. Add oil as needed. After 5 or 10 minutes of rubbing, have the person turn sunny-side up. Trace a fresh supply of oil into the person's midsection, then skip up to the shoulders and down to the thighs. Massage as long and sensually as you and your partner wish, but with one caution. Save massage of the breasts, nipples and genitals for last. Whether or not you progress into gentle teasing and fondling of your mate's sex organs depends on whether the two of you plan to have intercourse right after the massage. The choice is up to you.

5. *Sexual intercourse* after both of you have had a relaxing and tender massage is a truly exquisite experience. If you wish, you can leave enough oil on your skin to slip and slide on one another— guaranteed to produce tingles of excitement. The wife will be aroused and ready for intercourse because of the massage, and the bath oil will serve as a lubricant to add to her own natural vaginal oils. (A caution: if the two of you depend on a condom for birth control, you'll have to wipe the oil off the man's penis to keep the condom from slipping off.) You can use the sensual massage to build up to an exploration of your mate's body for new ways to build sexual excitement. If this is your goal, avoid massaging your partner's genital areas. Give a good massage to the non-genital areas, then go on to Step Three.

Step Three: Explore Your Mate's Body for New Ways to Build Sexual Excitement.

Masters and Johnson found that one reason many couples have sexual difficulties is that they've never stopped to explore the ways they can use to arouse one another. To reeducate these couples, Dr. Masters and Dr. Johnson developed the ''sensate focus'' exercises on which Step Three of the Sensual Union is based. Let me tell you about

The Couple Who Learned How to Have Better Sex by Starting Over

Rob and Kelly A., a couple in their mid-thirties, had lost their interest in sex. They still loved each other, but their sex life had become so monotonous that they scarcely bothered with it. This was a great disappointment to Kelly, who felt sexier than she had ever felt in her life. She relieved her sexual tensions through erotic fantasies and masturbation, but worried that unless she and Rob could reawaken their interest in one another, their marriage would fail. A physician suggested that the couple might benefit from a sex therapy clinic being held in a nearby medical center. The doctor arranged for the referral, Rob took several days off from work, and they went.

The therapy sessions began with an orientation meeting, where a doctor explained to Rob and Kelly and the other couples what they'd be doing over the next few days. Each couple gave a sex history and underwent a genital examination. Then, they were instructed in the sensate focus exercises developed by Masters and Johnson. A counselor met with them daily to discuss their progress, and to hear what each partner had learned about the other. The exercises called for absolutely no sexual intercourse during the first week, but Rob and Kelly couldn't wait. They made passionate love after the fourth session, and returned from the clinic fully satisfied with what they'd accomplished. ''What the course did,'' Kelly admitted, ''was show us how to have better sex by starting over. I don't think Rob and I will ever again get into the rut we were in before we learned how to give pleasure to each other.''

Discovering Your Mate's Sensual Parts

Lovemaking is fun! The goal is mutual pleasure, and any couple can achieve this when each partner makes an honest attempt to supply the other's needs. The purpose of sexual exploration is to find new ways to build sexual excitement. The seven-day outline that follows contains the sensate focus exercises developed by Masters and Johnson. The purpose of these exercises is to reawaken your interest in your mate—and his in you. However, any couple can enjoy these exercises. They will excite you, give you pleasure, and show you how to please your mate.

First, some rules. Set aside about an hour a day for a week so that you and your mate can have an uninterrupted session of talking and fondling. Take the phone off the hook, lock the bedroom door and insure yourselves complete privacy. (One advantage of going off to a therapy clinic is that in a motel or hotel you're more likely to have complete privacy, so you may wish to spend the week together in a motel.) Remove all clothing before beginning the exercises. Leave the lights on, but you can turn them down to a sexy shade. You may want to begin the exercises by bathing or showering together. Fine. Just don't touch one another's genitals. The purpose of the exercises is to learn how to arouse your mate in ways other than by stimulating the genitals. You may also wish to begin the exercises with a sensuous massage; if you do, avoid genital contact during the caressing. Lovemaking is the sum of many things: sight, touch, smell and other sensations. During these exercises, concentrate on feeling and seeing your partner's body.

DAY ONE: The husband takes a position sitting in the center of the bed with his back against the headboard. His wife sits between his legs. Her feet should rest on the outside of his legs, and her head can rest on his shoulder. She takes a passive role while her husband tries to give her pleasure by touching and fondling any part of her body except her breasts or genital areas. The husband's only goal is to give his wife pleasure and to enjoy touching and seeing his wife's body.

The wife doesn't touch her husband, but she must tell or show him what she likes. She can say, "That feels good," or she can guide his hand back to a pleasurable spot. Gradually, the husband will learn what she likes and what she doesn't like.

After 10 or 20 minutes, the husband and wife change places. She begins exploring every part of his body except his genitals. He tells her what he likes and what he doesn't like.

The exploration period lasts about half an hour, and at the end you and your mate should relax or go to sleep.

DAY TWO: Set aside thirty minutes when the two of you can be free from interruptions. Spend this time discussing the first day's explorations. Tell each other what gave you the most pleasure and why you liked it. Be tender with one another, but don't have sexual intercourse.

DAY THREE: This time the wife begins the session sitting behind her husband and giving him pleasure. She can apply a body oil as she strokes the parts that he likes, and he should use his hand to guide her to especially sensitive areas (but not the genitals!). After 10 or 15 minutes, they exchange places and the husband applies oil to his wife and fondles her pleasurable areas.

DAY FOUR: As on Day One, the husband is the first pleasuring partner. The difference is that today, as well as caressing the places he's already learned give pleasure to his wife, he touches and feels her genitals. He should pay special attention to the texture of his wife's main lips and inner thighs, note how she reacts to gentle stroking of her pubic hair. He may wish to apply a small amount of body oil to her genitals during the stroking. The partners change positions after 10 or 20 minutes, and the wife explores and strokes all of her husband's body, including his penis and scrotum. She should note the velvety surface of the glans, the crinkly sensitivity of the sac, the way the skin of the penis stretches taut during an erection.

DAY FIVE: The husband lies on his back on the bed, while his wife applies a body oil and begins a sensuous massage of the lower part of his trunk. She is free to touch and look at every part of his genitals. The purpose is to familiarize her with her husband's body. She may enjoy telling him what she sees, or how she feels about what she sees. After 10 to 20 minutes of exploration, the partners change places. The wife lies on her back and the husband becomes the explorer.

DAY SIX: No touch session today, just a talk in privacy between husband and wife about their reactions to Day Five. This is a good time to be completely truthful with one another about the parts of lovemaking you find most pleasurable. Be open with your mate, not critical. Show your love by sharing your knowledge of the lovemaking techniques you like best.

DAY SEVEN: Begin this session with a sensuous massage. Progress to genital exploration and stimulation, and let your partner do the same for you. Then, if you wish, have intercourse. It should be a thrilling climax to a week of sexual reawakening!

Step Four: Begin to Try New Things Together.

Sometimes a sexual difficulty can be traced to boredom. Husband and wife make love in the same way at the same time over and over until the act loses its excitement. To improve your Sensual Union, get out of your rut!

Get to know the person you're living with! Go out together once or twice a week—and go alone! No kids, no friends, just the two of you. Alternate picking what your activity will be. The only rule is that you do what he suggests when it's his time, and what she suggests when it's her time.

Put variety into your sex life. The best sex is spontaneous, not something that can be predicted as to time, method and position. To improve your Sensual Union, experiment with different techniques of intercourse, and lay the groundwork for having sex at unusual times and in unusual places. Some places you might want to have sex include:

1. On the bedroom floor
2. In the den
3. In the closet
4. In the bathroom

5. In the car
6. On top of the kitchen table
7. On the sofa
8. In the back yard

Of course, this is a very incomplete list of places to have sex; use your imagination to think of others. And have sex in the morning some of the time, or at noon, or before supper. Wake your partner for some good loving in the middle of the night.

Learning to Give and Receive Pleasure from Every Body Part

The Sensual Union is a way of giving pleasure to each other, and of making sex what it was meant to be: fun. Get in the habit of thanking your mate for a sexual gift. Say, "I enjoyed that," or "I liked that a lot," or "I'm crazy about you." And you can always go back to the best sentence of all: "I love you."

Pretty soon you'll find that you can give and receive pleasure from every part of your body. A touch of your fingertips can be a lovely thing, so can an embrace, a kiss, a wink or a smile of pleasure. Smiling is the language of love, and we all ought to do more of it. Your lips and tongue, in fact, are two of your sexiest parts. In the next chapter we'll take up the ways you can use these and other body parts to put some zip into your Sensual Union.

6

The Sensual
Union—Week Two

By now, you and your partner know more about one another's sensuality. You've learned what he or she likes, and may have discovered some things you particularly like. You've begun to do new things with your mate, put some fun into your sex life. The purpose of the second week of improving the Sensual Union is to continue this learning and teaching process.

Remember that lovemaking can take many forms, and that the goal is mutual pleasure. Some of the time you're the teacher, and at other times you're the student. Don't force anything on your partner, but do be willing to learn and discover together. Go at a pace that will give both of you sexual happiness and satisfaction. The steps in the second week of the Sensual Union are:

STEP FIVE: *Enjoy the Pleasure That Comes from Doing What Your Mate Likes.*

STEP SIX: *Fill Your Sensual Appetite with Something Good.*

STEP SEVEN: *Dress Up Your Sensual Union as Sexily as Possible.*

STEP EIGHT: *Heighten Your Sexual Enjoyment in Special Ways.*

Step Five: Enjoy the Pleasure That Comes from Doing What Your Mate Likes.

As human beings, we have certain things in common. We get pleasure from eating, from satisfying body urges, and from sexual relations. One thing that every person enjoys is intimate stimulation from his marriage partner. The stimulation can range from stroking to fondling to sexual intercourse. An enticing variation of the lovemaking technique is to stimulate your partner's body with the most erotic of your sexual organs.

The Most Erotic Sexual Organ in the Body

Your most erotic sexual organ is your mouth! A kiss can be a tantalizing, sensual experience, whether applied to the mouth or some other body part. The tongue is not only sensitive, it is a strong, well-coordinated muscle. You can lick with it, probe with it or use it to tantalize any part of your mate's body. This sensual technique can bring a new surge of excitement to marital relations.

How Julia Learned to Enjoy Sex by "Giving In"

Julia and Walter B. had been married for fourteen years before she gave in to her own urges one night and gently slid her head down over her husband's body and kissed his penis. It was an exciting moment for him and for her. Explaining her experience, Julia said, "It was like, once I did that, all the bad things I'd been taught about sex just left me. I thought, if it's that wonderful in the effect it has on Walter and me, it can't be bad. I asked my minister about it, and he said that anything the husband and wife find enjoyable is all right for them to do. And you know something? Expressing my love for my husband just opened the door for a lot of exciting things for us to do. I wouldn't say that our sex life was bad before we started this, but it's been ten times more exciting since then."

Julia's husband agreed. He was

The Man Who Said He Wanted to Make Up for Lost Time

Walter knew about "going down" on his wife, but like Julia, he'd never worked up his courage to introduce this technique into their lovemaking. Once she led the way, he willingly followed. He kissed her breasts, her nipples, her stomach and her inner thighs. To his surprise, he found that oral stimulation greatly excited and pleased Julia. The first time Walter used his tongue to kiss and caress his wife's vagina, she had an orgasm. She, in turn, wanted to give him the same form of pleasure. For several weeks, the couple preferred having their orgasms this way. They'd discovered a technique that gave both of them happiness, and Walter's only regret was that it had taken them fourteen years to discover mouth-genital contact. "But that's okay," he said. "We're making up for lost time."

Lovemaking Techniques That Please a Woman

A wife may enjoy many forms of sexual stimulation, but she'll probably admit that kissing of her body ranks near the top of the list. The husband should experiment to find the forms of kissing she likes best. Gradually he can learn to kiss and lick her breasts and nipples, and to work his way down so that his head is between her thighs. He might begin by snuggling a cheek against her pubic hair, or by applying light kisses to her inner thighs. How quickly he progresses to more intimate stimulation will depend on his wife's reaction and his own desires.

Mouth-genital stimulation of the mons, clitoris, inner lips and vagina is known as *cunnilingus*. Done slowly and sensually, this technique can bring great joy to the wife. In fact, it can also give much joy and satisfaction to the husband. The technique requires the efforts of both partners. With her hands the wife can guide her husband's mouth and show him what is pleasurable and what isn't. Licking and kissing of the outside parts may be all she wants or can tolerate at first. Eventually, the husband may want to put his tongue into the vagina and move it in and out as if it were his penis.

The vagina is a clean, natural body cavity that is neutral to pleasant in taste. In fact, most men find that the sexual scents of a woman are particularly exhilirating. Vaginal secretions are hardly different from saliva. The act itself, then, is one that is little different from an open-mouthed kiss. The husband can either crouch between his wife's thighs as she lies on her back on the bed, or he can kneel at the edge of the bed and draw her toward him. He can perform cunnilingus while lying beside her in bed, and she can turn her body so that she can stimulate him at the same time.

Some women are better able to have a sexual climax during cunnilingus than during sexual intercourse. The husband might want to continue the tongue-to-vagina stimulation until his wife has at least one orgasm, and then mount her for man on top sexual intercourse. Or, he can let her take the top position. He'll find that stimulating her with his tongue and mouth has given him more excitement than he expected, and that his wife's pitch of excitement may bring him quickly to orgasm during intercourse.

As with all lovemaking techniques, variation is important. The wife doesn't want mouth-genital stimulation every time, and certainly not to orgasm every time. But it is a lovemaking technique that pleases her and that can bring much joy to her husband.

Lovemaking Techniques That Please a Man

A man enjoys his wife's touches and kisses. His nipples are sensitive, and so are his fingertips and the skin of his chest and thighs. But most of his sexual sensations are centered in the penis. One of the most pleasing and loving things that a wife can do is to take her husband's penis into her mouth and gently suck it. A wife may find the thought of doing this unappealing. She shouldn't. The penis is a clean, muscular organ. It stands hard and erect, and taking it into the mouth is as natural as taking it into the vagina.

The act is known as *fellatio*, and it can be performed in many different positions. The wife can kneel or lie beside her husband or between his legs, or have him stand or sit on the bed while she takes a position in front of him. The most sensitive part of the penis is the glans, or head, and the wife should devote most of her attention to it. Sucking movements can be slow or fast, continuous or intermittent, shallow or deep. One thing to avoid is using the teeth, though light stroking of the penis with the teeth can be pleasant. Just under the glans is a delicate and very sensitive web of skin, the frenulum. A man enjoys having this licked or stimulated by his wife's tongue. His testicles, too, are sensitive, and some men like mouth-genital stimulation of the scrotum and its contents.

The duration of fellatio depends on the couple's desires. The husband who has his orgasm during fellatio is not going to be of much use in further stimulating his wife, at least not for awhile. It's best that the couple work out a way for the husband to tell his wife when it's time to stop—that is, before it's too late. By taking turns giving mouth-genital stimulation, the husband and wife can prolong their excitement for half an hour or more. Then, intercourse with the penis in the vagina becomes a thrilling event.

Sooner or later the husband may have his orgasm during fellatio. This is no tragedy. His wife may have already experienced one or more orgasms, or may get them during later lovemaking. The man's ejaculate totals about a teaspoonful of clear to cloudy liquid. It spurts out wet and sticky, but is practically tasteless. The wife may prefer to swallow it (it won't hurt you), spit it out, or stop the fellatio as soon as her husband begins to come. She should bear in mind that the spilling of his semen is very pleasurable to a man. It is more pleasurable when the entire ejaculation takes place inside the mouth. The wife who prefers to avoid semen can do so in a simple way. All she has to do is ask her husband to wear a condom during fellatio. A wife who is sucking a penis not ensheathed by a condom should be aware of one other thing. As a man's sexual excitement rises, a few drops of clear fluid may come out of his penis. This is not semen. It is a lubricating fluid secreted by the Cowper's glands at the base of the penis. Its release means that the man is thoroughly enjoying his wife's lovemaking technique, but not that he is ejaculating.

The Pleasure of Doing What Your Mate Likes

The biggest surprise of mouth-genital lovemaking is the pleasure it gives the partner who is doing the stimulating. Pleasure does come from giving! A man bringing his wife to orgasm by cunnilingus may find his own excitement hard to contain, and a wife who goes down on her husband may find that the act excites her and makes her sexually more responsive. The mouth, like the genitals, is capable of both giving and receiving pleasure.

Step Six: Fill Your Sensual Appetite with Something Good.

A variation of mouth-genital contact is the sensual meal. This is just what it sounds like. You apply something good to the mate's genitals, and then eat and lick it away! Your choice of food is limited only by your own likes and dislikes. However, it does need to be a warm and not a refrigerated food. Most couples prefer dessert type foods, such as meringue, fruit salad, instant pudding or tapioca. Dip works just as well. What's your favorite? Avocado? Bean dip? Light cheese dip? You can apply it around the penis or mons and use your tongue as the dipper. *Bon appetit!*

The Man Who Turned His Wife On in an Unusual Way

Acting on something that his wife told him, one man hit on an unusual and exciting way to turn her on. She told him that in some of her sexual fantasies she imagined herself staked out in the desert, her body covered with honey and her hands tied so that she couldn't keep the ants from coming after the honey. Then, her lover would miraculously appear to rescue her. After chasing the ants away, the lover would use his tongue to gently remove all traces of honey from her body.

The husband took the cue; he had his wife lie on her back on some towels, and poured honey over her breasts and lower stomach. Then he "rescued" her just the way the man in her fantasies had done. The wife loved it. She insisted on stimulating her husband in the same way. She whipped up some dessert topping and applied it around his penis until his love organ looked like a sundae. She topped the dessert with a cherry, and enjoyed it thoroughly. So did her husband. Afterwards, they concluded their lovemaking with intensely satisfying sexual intercourse.

Step Seven: Dress Up Your Sensual Union as Sexily as Possible.

Sexual fantasies occur to almost everyone. In these little dreams you see yourself in different sexual roles, either having sex with someone besides your mate, or having intercourse with your mate but in an unusual way. You'll be surprised at how much fun it can be to act out your sexual fantasies with your marriage partner. Let's look at how a wife can become every woman for her husband, and how a husband can become every man for his wife.

Three Ways to Become Every Woman for Your Husband

Wearing a costume doesn't change *you*, but it does change the way you look. It's a way of dressing up the Sensual Union, of becoming every woman for your husband. Here are three ways to do this:

1. *Try a change of costume.*
2. *Try being the aggressor.*
3. *Spice up your lovemaking technique with variety.*

1. Try a Change of Costume.

Remember that the simplest costumes are the best ones. You are the woman your husband loves. Choose something that will bring out your sexiest features. When your husband gets home this evening, meet him at the front door wearing a party dress (something slinky and low-cut), a new bathing suit, or hip-hugging tight pants. Surprise him at least once a week. Realize that the softer the garment, the more appealing it will be to a man. Thus, silk is sexier than denim, cotton is sexier than wool. Emphasize your lingerie. Buy a complete new set. Get bikini panties and low-cut bras. Ever thought about a bra with tassels on it? Don't ask your husband if he'd like you in one; try greeting him in one and find out for yourself. Any change in what you wear will excite your husband, and so will a change in how much you wear. In fact, your birthday suit can be the sexiest "costume" of all!

Margaret's Ten-Minute Way of Exciting Her Husband

Margaret, a tall, attractive brunette, had been married to Frank for ten years. Their sex life was okay, but Margaret wanted it to be more than that. There were times when she wanted sex and her husband didn't seem interested. She had noticed one thing. Frank had a tendency to stare at blond women. One afternoon Margaret stopped in a coiffure shop and purchased a blond wig. She also bought a sexy negligee and some eye shadow and false eyelashes. Back home, she practiced putting on the costume until she could make the change in ten minutes. She spent the rest of the afternoon planning the surprise for her husband. Her two children arrived home from school, and she took them to her mother's for supper and a visit. She was home, alone, when her husband got there at five-thirty. Margaret greeted him with a kiss and whispered that she had a surprise for him. While Frank settled down with the paper on the front sofa, Margaret disappeared into the back room. Ten minutes later she reappeared wearing the blond wig and negligee. Frank did a double-take and began chasing her around the davenport. The couple made love on the sofa—also a change for them—and Frank told his wife that her "ten-minute surprise" was the most exciting thing that had happened to him in years.

2. Try Being the Aggressor.

Trying out new costumes is one way of being the aggressor in the Sensual Union, but you can take the lead in other ways as well. Consider this. Like women, men have sexual fantasies. A fairly common one is for the man to see himself being "attacked" by a lovely woman—sometimes by more than one woman. Obviously you can't be more than one person, but you can take the lead in initiating sex. Let your husband be passive while you undress him and kiss him and maybe suck his penis until it is hard and throbbing for action! You might say, "This time, I'm going to get you," or "This one's all on me." Say whatever it takes to make his blood boil, but show him that a woman is every bit the sexual equal of a man!

I suggested this technique to one woman, but she resisted. "I'd be afraid to try that," she said, "because my husband might turn me down. And it would just floor me if he did." Fear of rejection is understandable, but it is a risk that, when he is the aggressor, the man must also take. The husband and wife who enjoy a Sensual Union have ways of communicating their desire for sex. Wait until you know that he wants it, and then give it to him. You might combine your aggressiveness with a costume. Leather and denim are materials that suggest power. Try calf-length boots, cut-off denim jeans and a bare chest. Or attack him while wearing nothing but one of his tee shirts.

3. Spice Up Your Lovemaking Technique with Variety.

Being the aggressor every now and then is one way of adding spice to the Sensual Union. Another way is to vary your lovemaking technique. Try new things with your hands, your mouth and other body parts. You can pinch, tweak, fondle, stroke, rub and knead your husband's body during lovemaking. Rub his back with your thighs, his face with your breasts. One thing that will please him is for you to pay attention to his penis. If it's limp, take it in your mouth and suck rather vigorously. If it's hard, use your mouth and tongue lightly at first, then with more determination. Surprise your man by insisting that you won't stop sucking his penis until he's had complete satisfaction. Sure, he'll ejaculate, and sure, his sexual excitement will die down for a quarter of an hour or longer. But you'll enjoy giving him what he likes, and you'll find that it will make him want to give you what you like. To repeat, the goal of sex is mutual pleasure. You and your husband need not have a simultaneous orgasm every time you make love. Do what is fun and what is natural for the two of you.

Three Ways to Become Every Man for Your Wife

Sex is a partnership, but some men tend to forget this. I read a letter to Dear Abby in which a man complained about his unresponsive wife and asked if Abby had an answer. Her reply was "What's the question?" She went on to explain that any woman can be turned on if her husband will go about it in the right way. The three ways that a husband can become every man to his wife are:

1. Dress up your act.
2. Try new things.
3. Spice up your technique.

1. Dress Up Your Act.

Most men find the idea of wearing a costume silly, and it may be. But your wife may have other ideas. She may envision a romantic scene where a virile young man wearing bathing tights makes passionate love to her. If you can play this role, try it. Some women have fantasies about men in a locker room or gymnasium. Sight of a man wearing only an athletic supporter may turn her on. Try it. One lady told me that the star character in her recurring fantasy was a burglar with a droopy mustache. The man was dressed in a suit jacket and tie, but wore nothing from the waist down. And though he came to steal the silverware, when he saw the sexy lady of the house he decided to steal something else. Learning of the fantasy, her husband acted the role of the burglar, and triggered a very erotic lovemaking session with his wife.

2. Try New Things.

Playing roles is a way of improving the Sensual Union. Perhaps the most familiar sexual scenario is the game "Doctor," played by many children by the time they're school age. Adults can enjoy this, too. You may or may not want to purchase a white smock and a doctor's bag, but you can turn an "examination" into a sensual massage and an exciting sexual experience. A college English professor and his wife invented their own games. Both were avid readers, and they were

The Couple Who Put Sex Scenes into Their Marriage

Soon after they were married, Richard and Jessica discovered that they both enjoyed a rich fantasy life. They liked to read sexy books together, and to act out the parts of the main characters. "We read a lot of new stuff, but even though what we do is unusual, Jessica and I are both old-fashioned," Richard told me. "We tend to go back and do the same scenes over and over. Jessica's favorite is that scene in *Peyton Place* where the young girl goes off to a cabin with a man from New York. She also likes two or three different places in the book *Lady Chatterly's Lover*, especially that part where the gardener makes a big fuss over Lady Chatterly's pubic hair. My favorite has always been that very first lovemaking scene between Sergeant Warden and Karen Holmes in *From Here to Eternity*. You may recall that's the place where she looks at him with eyes of liquid smoke, removes her shorts and dares him to take her—which, of course, he does. We've done that one dozens of times, and never tire of it.''

Playing roles is exciting because it combines erotic fantasies, imagination and costuming. You don't have to read books to enjoy role-playing. Write your own script. Your wife may enjoy being "picked up" by a strange man—you! Let her dress up in some wild outfit and go alone to a nightspot. A little later, drop by the same place and pick her up. But don't take her home. Take her to a motel. Make passionate love to her, and then talk her into going home to share your bed for some more lovemaking.

Lead the way in showing new things for the two of you to do. Make love in your car on a hill overlooking the city. Or take her into the back yard or to a private place and make love under the stars. Make love in a hammock, in the shower, in the bathtub, in a swimming pool or in the kitchen. Try new things, and you'll reap the rewards!

3. Spice Up Your Technique.

Dr. Kinsey's studies show that most American men do not spend enough time on the excitement phase of sexual intercourse. Your wife's responsiveness, as a rule, will mirror your own ability as a lover. Slow down. Be a sexual gourmet, and enjoy every part of the love act. Try, now and then, to see how long you and your wife can spend in the foreplay leading up to insertion. Learn the textures and nuances of your wife's body. Touch her and fondle her and stroke her and kiss her. Luxuriate in the fine oil of her vagina. Dip a finger into it and spread the oil around her labia. Or spread it with your tongue. If she wants, give her cunnilingus. Do it until your jaw aches too much to continue, or until she's had so many orgasms she's exhausted.

Be aware of the different positions for sexual intercourse (Chapter 2). At least every other time you make love, let your wife choose the position. You may want to begin intercourse standing up, then try various positions in bed. Let her take the top. This is the one position where her excitement will proceed as rapidly as yours. Later, you can take the top, or you and your wife can enjoy intercourse side by side. Enter her from the rear; she'll find this exciting and so will you. One shortcut to a Sensual Union is to never make love exactly the same way two times in a row!

Step Eight: Heighten Your Sexual Enjoyment in Special Ways.

Three ways to heighten your sexual enjoyment are to have anal intercourse and to use a dildo and a vibrator to give the wife pleasure. Of course, lovemaking is so varied an art that what one couple enjoys may not be suitable for another couple. You don't have to do any of the things in Step Eight to enjoy a Sensual Union, but you may find them exciting and pleasurable.

A Form of Loving That Can Please a Man

A special form of intercourse, anal intercourse, can be an exciting variation of the Sensual Union. Some couples enjoy it, while others don't. It is apt to please the man who takes a special interest in the soft fullness of his wife's hips, and it can thrill a woman as well. However, several precautions are necessary.

The position is that of rear entry. The wife rests on her stomach on top of a pillow, or she can kneel on her hands and knees. Her husband mounts from behind, and gently inserts his penis into her anus. The key word is "gentle." The anus is the muscular opening to the rectum, and it will admit an erect penis. Even so, entry may be painful to a woman, especially if done too quickly or without lubrication. Do not attempt it if it causes discomfort. The best form of lubrication is for the man to wear a premoistened condom. Wearing a condom helps in other ways. Most couples make anal intercourse only one phase of their lovemaking, and go on to vaginal intercourse afterwards. By wearing a condom and then stripping it off, the man can avoid transferring rectal germs to his wife's vagina. (If needed for birth control, he can pull on another condom before inserting his penis into the vagina.) Once entry is achieved, gentle back and forth thrusts of the penis can be done in the same way as during vaginal intercourse.

The only reasons not to have anal intercourse are when either partner doesn't want to, or when the wife has any medical condition involving her anus or a history of having had hepatitis. (Hepatitis is a disease that can be passed through the stools and rectal contents, and the husband would run the risk of contracting it.)

Special Ways of Pleasing a Woman

The vagina is a woman's love organ. Its entrance and the lips around it are richly supplied by sensitive nerve endings. The penis stimulates these nerves during intercourse, but so can many other things. The husband's fingers, for example, are particularly suited to exploring the depths of the vagina. One or two fingers moved back and forth in the vagina after the wife is aroused can be a sensual form of lovemaking. The husband may prefer to combine the technique with stimulation of his wife's clitoris. If so, he should use a gentle rubbing motion over the mons and main lips. A variation of using the fingers to stimulate the vagina is to use a dildo. It is an artificially erect penis made of rubber, plastic or wood. So long as the husband lubricates it and is gentle with it, the dildo can be a sensuous addition to his lovemaking technique.

The Man Who Found Just What He Was Looking for in the Kitchen

One of my patients gave me some advice on how to improve the Sensual Union between a man and his wife. He hit on the idea of using a dildo that he found in an unusual place—the kitchen. Late one evening while he and his wife were baking a cake, he noticed that one of her aluminum cake molds was shaped remarkably like the first three or four inches of the penis (though it was somewhat larger in diameter). He began to tease his wife about using it on her, and the two of them found the thought extremely erotic. They retired to the bedroom, and at the height of his wife's excitement, the man gently inserted the cake mold into her vagina. She had an immediate orgasm—the first of many in a long and pleasurable session of lovemaking.

I thanked the patient for his idea, and would like to carry it one step further by mentioning that the average household contains many items that can be used for vaginal stimulation. A cucumber is one, a wiener or sausage another. Look around, and use what is available. Just don't insert into the vagina anything but a very smooth, non-injurious item. Certain specialty shops sell dildos, and an even more stimulating device, the vibrator, is available in just about any drugstore or novelty shop.

Vibrators come in different sizes and shapes. The item was originally meant for giving massages, and its various attachments can be used for gentle or vigorous stimulation of the skin. An ordinary vibrator applied to the main lips, mons and clitoris can greatly excite a woman. The man applies the stimulation under his wife's guidance. A cordless vibrator that can be inserted into the vagina is on the market. It gets its power from a battery, has a smooth, cone-shaped surface, and is several inches long. Used properly, it can provide the ultimate in genital stimulation for a woman.

Lovemaking Techniques That Can Please Both Partners

Lovemaking should be fun, and the way to improve the Sensual Union is to use any technique that pleases both partners. The best technique is a combination of all the methods discussed in Steps One through Eight. The eight steps in the Sensual Union are:

STEP ONE: Put Some Fun into Sex.

STEP TWO: Benefit from the Joys of a Sensuous Massage.

STEP THREE: Explore Your Mate's Body for New Ways to Build Sexual Excitement.

STEP FOUR: Begin to Try New Things Together.

STEP FIVE: Enjoy the Pleasure that Comes from Doing what Your Mate Likes.

STEP SIX: Fill Your Sensual Appetite with Something Good.

STEP SEVEN: Dress up Your Sensual Union as Sexily as Possible.

STEP EIGHT: Heighten Your Sexual Enjoyment in Special Ways.

Find new sexual enjoyment by trying new things! Begin lovemaking with a sensuous massage, and go on to other techniques. The husband might give his wife cunnilingus, then don a condom for a short session of anal intercourse. They might then want to have vaginal intercourse to mutual orgasm. The next time they might prefer to have intercourse standing in front of a mirror, or have fellatio followed by vaginal stimulation with a dildo or vibrator. Still another time they might prefer a "quickie" under the kitchen table, or a sensuous hour of lovemaking in front of a roaring fire. There need be no limit to the variety and sequence of lovemaking techniques, and this is why the Sensual Union is one that grows and grows.

The Sensual Union That Grows and Grows

Someone has said that a good wife doesn't get older—she gets better! The same is true of a good husband. Just realize that each couple must proceed at their own rate in developing the pleasure-giving techniques of the Sensual Union. I've given this as a two-week program, but it need have no upper time limit. The Sensual Union grows and grows, and that's why it gets better with the passage of years. In a sense, lovemaking is like life. It needn't proceed straight from point A to point B. It has its little detours, its ups and downs.

The techniques of the Sensual Union are reinvigorating ones, meant to improve the sexual side of marriage by showing new things you and your mate can enjoy. Do just that—enjoy them. Proceed at whatever rate will make both of you happy.

A Sensuous Union can make sex fun, exciting, and a source of deep pleasure. On the other hand, some couples may find that they still lack the ability to enjoy sex together. Many things may be responsible for this. Maybe the husband has trouble getting an erection—or ejaculates too quickly. Or maybe the wife never has an orgasm, yet wants one very much. We'll look at these and other problems in the next chapter, "Overcoming Problem Areas in the Sexual Relationship."

7

Overcoming Problem Areas in the Sexual Relationship

In the chapters on the Sensual Union, I emphasized how you can get more out of marriage by trying new things and concentrating on the pleasures of sex. However, some couples have problems that prevent them from enjoying sex. My purpose in this chapter is to discuss these problem areas and show how it is possible to overcome them. The specific topics are:

1. The man who has trouble achieving an erection.
2. The man who ejaculates too quickly.
3. The woman who doesn't reach a climax.
4. The woman who experiences pain during intercourse.
5. Other sexual problems.

Recognizing a Problem When it Exists

Most couples wait too long to seek help for a sexual problem. Later in this chapter I'll present the case of a 30-year-old woman named Susan. She and her husband had been married for seven years, yet had never had sexual intercourse. A specialist solved

Susan's problem and the couple were able to enjoy a happy sexual adjustment. Their case is not unique. Some couples begin marriage with the notion that intercourse is carried on by moving the penis back and forth between the woman's tightly closed thighs. Others think that the only time a couple can have relations is during her menstrual period, while still others are hindered by the belief that sexual pleasure is for men only. Probably the most common problem is pure boredom; the husband and wife make love in the same way for so long that they simply lose interest in sex.

The first thing for the sexually troubled couple to do is to get the difficulty out in the open. Discuss it! Realize that by working together, you can solve it. Of course, it may not be easy to recognize that a problem exists. If your sex life is fun and rewarding, if both of you look forward to sex as a pleasant and exciting way of sharing your love, then things are okay. However, if sex isn't fun, or is dreaded rather than anticipated, you have a problem. Recognize it and do something about it! Marriage is a partnership, which means sharing the good things as well as the problems. The end result, sexual happiness, is well worth the effort required to achieve it.

1. The Man Who Has Trouble Achieving an Erection.

Impotence, the failure to get or keep an erection, is the most common sexual problem of men. It can have many causes. Bear in mind that a woman is physically able to have intercourse at any time, even when she's not in the mood. A man, by contrast, must first achieve an erection, and hardening of the penis is a body reaction over which he has no direct control. He can't command himself to have an erection and expect one to automatically appear, simply because the event itself is a reflex. The nervous system must react in a certain way, and bring on corresponding changes in the blood vessels to the penis. Sexual excitement gets things started. In the man who is relaxed and in good health, more blood will enter his penis than will leave it, and the organ will get hard.

Almost every man can recall a time when he failed to achieve an erection in spite of wanting to very much. This can be embarrassing, but it is usually temporary and no cause for alarm. Impotence that becomes a problem is another matter. Perhaps the man can achieve an erection every second or third time that he tries, but he's never sure on a given occasion that he will be able to perform. He tends to lose confidence in himself, which adds to the problem. At least 80% of men bothered by impotence can be cured. The first step is to find the cause of the erection failure. It may be a physical disease, a drug, or a psychological disturbance.

How Arthur Overcame His Impotence

Arthur, a 60-year-old salesman, developed impotence that gradually worsened over a three-year period. He confided his problem to a friend, who advised him not to see a doctor. "They'll tell you that it's in your head. What you need is a different woman." The friend suggested seeing a prostitute, but Arthur wouldn't. He knew that a loss of interest wasn't the cause for his problem. He desired his wife very much, but just couldn't achieve an erection. Finally, he visited a doctor.

The physician discovered that the arteries to Arthur's penis were severely diseased. The blood circulation to his penis was almost nil. After vascular surgery was successful in restoring Arthur's pelvic blood flow, his ability to have an erection returned. He and his wife were able to resume their sexual relations.

The outcome in Arthur's case was a happy one. On the other hand, he waited too long to seek help. Visit a physician for help if you regularly have trouble having an erection. Among the conditions the doctor will search for are:

- *Blood vessel disease*
- *Diabetes mellitus*
- *Spinal cord disease (or injury)*
- *Infection such as tuberculosis, mumps or venereal disease*

- *Thyroid and other glandular diseases*
- *Disease of the blood or lymphatics*
- *Disease or past surgery of the prostate*
- *Drug ingestion*

Drugs That Can Cause Impotence

Drugs that affect the nervous system can cause impotence. Thus, tranquilizers, sleeping pills, speed (stimulants), narcotics, marijuana and blood pressure pills can cause a failure of erection. Probably the most common cause of temporary impotence is a drug people don't consider as such: alcohol. Alcohol is indeed a drug, and drinking can cause impotence. Avoiding alcohol will enable the man to return to his normal sexual role. Sometimes the causative drug is one prescribed by a doctor.

The Drug Clarence Took
That Caused Two Things to Go Down

Clarence R., a 50-year-old banker, developed high blood pressure and was put on the drug reserpine as treatment. Reserpine did lower Clarence's blood pressure, but it also took away his ability to have an erection. Clarence was inclined to blame the problem on his age, but his wife had other notions. She insisted he go back to the doctor. Clarence did, and the doctor apologized for not having mentioned that reserpine might cause impotence. He prescribed a different medicine for the patient's high blood pressure, and soon Clarence and his wife were enjoying their normal frequency of sexual relations.

Psychological Reasons for Impotence

Anything that affects a man's life can affect his sexual performance. He may have trouble achieving an erection when he's tired, upset, or sick. Depression is a common, but overlooked, cause of impotence. Things may not be going well at work, or the man may have financial problems or be upset because of the illness or death of a relative. The surge of freedom and happiness that occurs during a vacation can work wonders when the man's problem is fatigue due to overwork. Having some free time may revitalize both his interest in sex and his ability to perform. Still another cause of impotence is a feeling of guilt.

The Cure Nick Found for His Impotence

Nick, a 27-year-old auto salesman, developed impotence and came in for an appointment. He dated the onset of his problem to an afternoon four months previously when an attractive young woman came in to look at a sports car. The lady made her willingness known to Nick, and the two had intercourse that same afternoon. It was Nick's first infidelity, and he regretted it immediately. He rushed home to take his wife out to dinner. Afterwards he tried to have sex with her, but couldn't achieve an erection. He hadn't been able to have intercourse with his wife since then.

Guilt was the cause of Nick's impotence, and I suggested that he tell his wife about the affair and ask her forgiveness. He told me that he'd been considering doing just that, and was glad to hear my suggestion. In a phone call a few days later, Nick sounded much happier. He told me that his wife had been very forgiving, and that things were definitely "looking up."

Four Ways a Wife Can Improve Her Husband's Performance

A wife can help her husband to overcome impotence. In fact, solving this problem can draw the couple closer together and give them a more loving relationship. Four ways to do this are:

- *Set the mood.* Don't make love unless both of you are in the mood. Do it when you're relaxed and happy. Play mood music, and give yourself an hour or more of uninterrupted privacy.

● *Relieve the pressure.* It's very important that the man feel at ease and under no pressure to perform. His wife's most loving gift at this time is her understanding. If she can convey the impression that she's happy just being with her husband and doesn't need to have intercourse for any greater enjoyment, then she can relieve him of the pressure of having to perform.

● *Stimulate the penis.* A back-and-forth motion of the foreskin over the glans is the usual method of stimulation a man employs during masturbation, but his wife may prefer to lick the penis, suck it, or rub it with her thighs or nipples. She should concentrate on giving her husband pleasure.

● *Stimulate the wife.* Her efforts to stimulate the penis will no doubt arouse the wife. She should tell her husband of her excitement, and let him feel (or taste) the oiliness of her vagina and the goose bumps on her nipples. It's time, then, for the man to help stimulate her to orgasm. He can choose any of the ways mentioned in the Sensual Union. Stimulating the wife will relieve her sexual tension, and it may bring on the husband's erection. If he does achieve an erection, the couple can conclude the lovemaking session with mutually satisfying sexual intercourse.

2. The Man Who Ejaculates Too Quickly.

The man who ejaculates before his wife is satisfied can deprive her of the full pleasure of sex. The man who can accomplish five or ten minutes of vaginal intercourse without an ejaculation doesn't have a problem, but the man who comes as soon as he enters the vagina does. Premature ejaculation exists when the man can't continue thrusting motions for more than a minute without reaching an orgasm. The condition is a frustrating one, but in most instances it can be corrected.

Freddie's Discovery of a Way to Give His Wife Sexual Satisfaction

Machismo was an important part of Freddie's personality. He was a Chicano who grew up in a rough section of San Antonio. He and his friends frequented prostitutes when he was a teen-ager, and the manly thing was to have an ejaculation as quickly as possible. The prostitute encouraged this practice, because it let her make more money in a given period of time. Eventually, Freddie stopped going to prostitutes. He finished a year in college, got a job with the telephone company, and married a pretty nurse's aide who worked in a large hospital.

Maria, Freddie's wife, had no sexual experiences before her marriage. Her husband excited and pleased her, but his passion built to a bursting point much too quickly. In fact, Freddie would usually ejaculate at the very moment of vaginal insertion. This left Maria unsatisfied. Gradually she began to find reasons to avoid having sex. Freddie couldn't understand her reluctance. He considered himself an excellent lover, and he was always tremendously satisfied by his sexual experiences. "Yes," Maria told him, "but most of what we do is for your enjoyment. A woman is different, and I'd like it if our lovemaking lasted longer."

They visited a marriage counselor, who explained that together they could work through the problem and have a better sex life. He outlined a specific program for controlling Freddie's premature ejaculation. He told them to relax and undress as if they were going to make love. Then, Maria was to stimulate Freddie's penis. Freddie would tell her when he was getting too excited, and she'd stop her stimulation and squeeze his penis just below the glans. The squeeze technique, developed by Masters and Johnson, had the effect of delaying Freddie's orgasm. After Freddie's excitement died down slightly, Maria would begin again to stimulate his penis, being careful to stop when he told her that he was becoming very excited. She applied the squeeze technique three times in their first session, and didn't quite make it in time on the fourth try. Nevertheless, the sessions soon taught Freddie how to recognize his rapid rise in sexual excitement and how to control it by having his wife apply the squeeze technique.

After two months of treatment, Freddie was able to have intercourse for several minutes; within six months he was able to continue intercourse long enough for his wife to have an orgasm. This was an extremely happy moment for Freddie. He told the counselor that he loved his wife more than ever now that he could satisfy her completely.

How to Control Premature Ejaculation

The squeeze technique is an effective way to control premature ejaculation. The correct place to squeeze the penis is just beneath the glans. The wife should put her thumb at the front of the penis over the web of skin (frenulum), and her index and middle fingers at the back of the penis just below the glans. The squeeze should be applied for 3 or 4 seconds on signal from the husband. A man doesn't know for sure that he is about to ejaculate until a few seconds before it begins. However, if he allows himself to reach the point of no return the squeeze technique won't stop the ejaculation. He should signal his wife to apply the squeeze when he feels that his excitement is getting out of control. The wife may worry that the squeeze will be painful to her husband. Usually, it isn't. He can guide her fingers to show the amount of pressure that is effective and painless.

Begin the lovemaking session with the husband on his back or sitting up in bed, and the wife in front of him. She alternately stimulates and squeezes the penis under his direction. The man may lose a little of his erection after each squeeze, but will quickly gain it back. Four or five squeezes a session are usually adequate, but a few more than this won't hurt.

It's best for the couple not to attempt intercourse until the husband can postpone his ejaculation for at least a ten- or fifteen-minute session of the squeeze technique. By then, he should be able to recognize the signs of his approaching ejaculation, and enlist his wife's help in postponing it. Intercourse is accomplished in a special way. First, the wife stimulates and squeezes her husband's penis two or three times. She then assumes the woman on top position and gently inserts the penis into her vagina. No thrusting is attempted. The couple remain motionless, and if the man feels that he's about to ejaculate, his wife can remove the penis from the vagina and apply the squeeze technique. In this manner the husband and wife can progress to the point of having thrusting motions and mutually enjoyable intercourse. Later, they can experiment with intercourse in different positions. The wife may still have to apply the squeeze technique if the husband becomes too excited too quickly. Several months or a year of working together may be necessary for completely successful results. Incidentally, a man cannot achieve control over premature ejaculation by applying the squeeze technique on himself. It takes his wife's help.

Other Methods of Prolonging a Man's Excitement

Some men who don't ejaculate prematurely do want to control their sexual excitement for a longer period of time. To some extent, aging will allow this. A man of 50 may not be as hot-blooded as he was at 20, but he'll probably be able to have intercourse for a much longer session than when he was in his twenties. Some methods that a man can use to hold off his climax are:

- *Wear a condom.* The condom cuts down on the sensitivity of intercourse. Wearing one may allow you to prolong the length of intercourse and delay your orgasm. The skin, or membrane condoms are the most sensitive, so a latex condom is preferable when the purpose is to prolong the session of lovemaking.
- *Use an anesthetic ointment.* Local anesthetic ointments such as Nupercainal can be purchased without a prescription, and more potent ones can be obtained with a doctor's prescription. Apply the anesthetic to the glans of the penis just before beginning intercourse. By reducing the sensitivity of the penis, the anesthetic can prolong the time before ejaculation. An additional benefit is that the anesthetic ointments have an oil base, which helps when vaginal lubrication is needed.

● *Practice mind control.* It's possible to put off an orgasm by deliberately thinking of something else when your level of excitement nears its peak. The trick is to change thoughts quickly while not changing your sexual performance. When your tide of excitement begins to ease, return your thoughts to the lovemaking.

3. The Woman Who Doesn't Reach a Climax.

A man must have an orgasm to release his seed, but a woman can get pregnant and bear children without ever enjoying the thrill of a sexual climax. Nature seems to have meant things this way. Slower sexual responsiveness on the part of the woman makes her the sexual superior to the man. Once he has his climax, a man's ardor dies down and he'll be out of action for a quarter of an hour or even a day or longer. Not so a woman. She could continue having sex with other men, which would increase her chances of becoming pregnant. Pregnancy—the continuance of our species—is a very important biologic event.

Even so, a woman can and should enjoy sex, including the sexual climax. A woman who never reaches a climax during intercourse is said to be "frigid." The term implies, further, that the woman is incapable of having an orgasm. The thing to remember is that "incapable" is a relative word. Helen Keller was "incapable" of speaking—until she was taught to do so by Anne Sullivan. American women were "incapable" of helping during wartime—until Clara Barton founded the Red Cross. Words such as "incapable" don't have any place in describing a woman's abilities or her sexual makeup. As one physician put it, "Most textbooks used to say that normal women did not enjoy sex. Most textbooks used to say that normal women did not have orgasms. Most textbooks used to be written by men."[1] It's now known that every woman is capable of having orgasms if she is stimulated in the right way.

---

[1] M. Weisberg, "Sexual Medicine," *The New Physician*, February, 1977, p. 43.

The Myth of the "Frigid Wife"

Earlier in this chapter I described the case of Freddie, the man who was bothered by premature ejaculation. Until he and his wife sought counseling, Freddie didn't think that he had a problem. He thought that his wife, Maria, was "frigid." Freddie came to this conclusion because he didn't understand the differences in the sexual responsiveness of a man and of a woman. He thought that Maria couldn't respond, when the real problem was that Maria wasn't given enough to respond to! In fact, a very common cause of a woman not enjoying sex is that her husband doesn't spend the time and give her the care she needs to have an orgasm. Behind the myth of the "frigid wife" is usually a husband whose lovemaking technique consists of "roll on, finish, roll off." The problem can be a frustrating one, and the only way for the wife to achieve satisfaction is for her and her husband to work together toward a solution.

Six Ways to Increase a Woman's Sexual Responsiveness

Six ways a husband and wife can work together to help her get more pleasure out of sex are:

a. *Discuss the problem openly and honestly.*
b. *Remove performance demands from the wife.*
c. *Explore the mate's body for new ways to build sexual excitement.*
d. *Don't begin vaginal intercourse until the wife is thoroughly aroused.*
e. *Search for the best lovemaking techniques.*
f. *Let the wife discover specific ways of increasing her responsiveness.*

a. Discuss the Problem Openly and Honestly.

The husband may not be aware that his wife isn't enjoying sex. She may be afraid to act otherwise in the belief that if she doesn't seem to like sex, her husband will stop making love to her and any chance of sexual enjoyment will be lost. An open, honest discussion is much better than pretense. The benefits to expect can be shown by

The Secret Cynthia Learned
about Her Sexual Responsiveness

Cynthia M., a 28-year-old woman, had been married for five years and had two children. Yet, she had never reached an orgasm during her marriage. She said that she loved her husband, Ed, and that during two episodes of intercourse with him before marriage she'd been completely satisfied. But beginning with their wedding night, the zip had gone out of their sex. She went on to disclose that she'd had intercourse with other men before her marriage, and that the lovemaking had usually led to an orgasm. Love within the bonds of marriage just wasn't exciting for Cynthia. Talking to her, I discovered that her past had contributed to her present difficulty.

Her mother had warned her that sex was bad, and spent many hours trying to convince Cynthia that if she let a boy touch her the next thing she knew she'd be pregnant or have venereal disease. Cynthia rebelled against her mother. She found boys fascinating and very desirable. She let them touch her, let them kiss her, let them make love to her. Her promiscuous sex life continued until she fell in love with Ed. They married, and Cynthia's five years of sexual frustration began.

Cynthia admitted that she had erotic fantasies about men other than her husband, and that she found the thought of an affair "exciting." The more she talked, the clearer it became that she associated enjoyable sex with "forbidden fruit." So long as the sex was outside the bonds of marriage, it was thrilling and satisfying. Once the act was permitted as a part of marriage, it lost its appeal. In fact, Cynthia was still rebelling against her mother, who used to beat her and hide her clothes to keep her from going out with boys. Helping Cynthia to recognize the source of her problem was the first part of treatment. Explaining her feelings to her husband was the next.

Cynthia dreaded my doing this, but she needn't have. Her husband was very supportive.

Ed told me that he loved his wife for what she was and what she meant to him, and that he was willing to do whatever was necessary to make her happy. Indeed, he had a suggestion. He thought that he could introduce a forbidden element into their sex by posing as a stranger and making sexual advances to his wife. I told him it was worth a try. Ed borrowed a set of overalls from a friend, and showed up at the door as a repairman. Cynthia asked him in, and soon they were in bed together. Another time he met her in a singles bar and took her to a nearby motel. Each time, Cynthia reached an orgasm. The couple worked out a series of sexual costumes and roles similar to those discussed in Step Seven of the Sensual Union, and Cynthia has been much happier in her relations with Ed. Even so, I referred her to a psychiatrist for further therapy, so that one day she'll be able to enjoy sex with Ed just because he is her husband and she loves him.

b. Remove Performance Demands from the Wife.

Beware of a potential hazard! The husband may be an achievement-oriented individual. Once he learns that his wife isn't reaching a climax, he may become so concerned about her feelings that he worsens the problem. How? By asking her right after lovemaking if she reached a climax. The stress of feeling that one has to have an orgasm can, itself, take the fun out of sex. An observant husband can tell when his wife is enjoying sex. He doesn't have to ask. By the same token, insisting that the wife have an orgasm is precisely the wrong thing to do. It's much better for the husband to show by his love and understanding that he wants his wife to enjoy sex as much as he does. By making their goal mutual pleasure, the couple can set a relaxed, non-demanding pace for their lovemaking. The woman stands a much better chance of fully appreciating sex under these circumstances.

c. Explore the Mate's Body for New Ways to Build Sexual Excitement.

Walt Disney was fond of saying that Disneyland would never be complete, because new and better features would continue to be added. I'd like to paraphrase Walt by saying that a husband's skill as a lover should never reach the point where he stops trying to learn new ways to please his wife. In fact, the best lovers are the ones who continually strive for improvement. A good idea might be to review Step Three of the Sensual Union, and start over in an exploration of the wife's body for new ways to generate sexual excitement. The goal is to discover the best techniques for arousing her. Together the husband and wife can learn to do the things that she likes and to avoid the things that she doesn't like.

d. Don't Begin Vaginal Intercourse Until the Wife is Thoroughly Aroused.

For a woman, entry of the penis into the vagina is one of the most ecstatic moments of intercourse—provided she is fully aroused. The husband who goes in too soon runs two risks. He may deprive her of the pleasure of entry, and he may race ahead to have his own orgasm before she reaches hers. A loving husband should learn to stimulate his wife until she practically begs him to put it in. Then, insertion of the penis and the subsequent intercourse will be thoroughly satisfying.

e. Search for the Best Lovemaking Techniques.

Try various positions for intercourse, and use more than one each time you make love. The top position gives a woman the most stimulation. She's free to move as she wishes and to control the rhythm of coitus. When he is in control, the husband should vary the speed of his thrusting. A stop and start, irregular motion is best during the early part of intercourse, but firm, regular strokes are more stimulating as the woman nears her climax. She can tell her husband what to do, or use her hands and body to show him what she likes. At the moment of his wife's orgasm, the husband should keep his penis deep inside the vagina. Her climax may last longer than his, and she should get the full enjoyment of it. The couple may find that it makes for a better climax to pause several times during the lovemaking session. The pause will take the edge off the husband's excitement, helping him not to ejaculate too quickly. At the same time, during a short pause a wife's excitement may stay the same or actually increase.

f. Let the Wife Discover Specific Ways of Increasing Her Responsiveness.

Dr. Kinsey showed that a woman who can masturbate to orgasm is more likely to have climaxes during sexual intercourse. Self-stimulation won't hurt you, and can teach you many things about your body's responsiveness. The mons, clitoris and inner thighs are very excitable. Stimulate these areas by massaging or rubbing them. Stimulation of the skin above and beside the clitoris is generally more enjoyable than direct massage of the organ. Some women enjoy masturbation in front of a mirror, though the more common position is to stretch out on the bed in the dark. Use of a vibrator is another way of increasing sexual responsiveness; most women who have tried one agree that a vibrator produces a more intense degree of stimulation than can be obtained by anything short of sexual intercourse. The vibrator can be the ordinary kind sold in drugstores and department stores, or a battery-operated one that is smooth, conical and pointed at one end like a penis. The woman should experiment to find the vibrator technique that works best for her. As an alternative, her husband can help her find the best ways to increase her responsiveness (see Step Eight of the Sensual Union).

4. The Woman Who Experiences Pain During Intercourse.

One of three things is usually responsible for a woman having pain during intercourse. Her vaginal opening may be too small to comfortably admit the penis, she may not have enough natural oils, or she may have a vaginal infection.

● *A snug opening* can cause pain when the husband tries to have intercourse before his wife is thoroughly aroused. Sexual excitement causes the vagina to enlarge, and this was demonstrated in the studies of Masters and Johnson. These researchers noted that when she was sexually excited, a woman with a small vagina could accommodate either a large or a small penis. However, attempts at intercourse before the woman reached the plateau phase of excitement were painful. A woman with a small vaginal opening may develop an additional problem: a spasm of the pelvic muscles that is known as *vaginismus*. Medical treatment is necessary. Consider

Susan's Seven-Year Problem

Susan was 30 and had been married for seven years, but she and her husband, John, had never had sexual intercourse. Susan's vaginal opening was so small that any attempt at intercourse was painful to her. She had become very unyielding to John's advances, and when she visited two physicians she resisted their attempts to examine her. A third doctor, a specialist in women's problems, found that Susan's vagina was normal except for the small entrance and for the fright the patient showed at being examined. Surgical enlargement of the opening wasn't necessary. Instead, the physician prescribed dilations of the vaginal opening using gradually larger metal dilators. During weekly office visits, the doctor's nurse assisted Susan in the dilations. Another thing Susan did was to begin using vaginal tampons instead of Kotex; this practice helped to enlarge her vaginal entrance. Gradually, Susan's problem was corrected. The final step in her treatment was to show her how to gently ease her husband's penis into her vagina. In the words of her physician, "After Susan learned to insert a dilator she learned to insert a penis.''[2] She and her husband began having enjoyable sexual relations, and were still doing well several months later. Still, Susan should not have waited so long to get help for her problem, and neither should you.

When spasm of the pelvic muscles is the main problem, the physician will try to uncover the cause. Sexual abuse during childhood can cause a woman to have this condition. The treatment begins with an understanding of the problem so that the husband and wife can work together toward a solution. Vaginal dilation with gradually larger metal dilators is curative. In fact, the husband and wife can make this a sensual experience by employing it in the privacy of their bedroom. Most therapists agree that the woman's vaginal entrance should be enlarged to where she can easily accommodate a dilator larger than her husband's penis before the couple attempt to have intercourse.

• *Lack of enough oils* need not mean that a woman has anything wrong with her. The problem may be that she isn't fully aroused, or that she's temporarily dry. For example, some women notice that they produce less vaginal oil during the week after a menstrual period (natural sex hormone levels are lower at this time). Persistent dryness is fairly easy to correct. The man should take the responsibility for providing extra lubrication, since the best place to apply it is to the head of the penis. Saliva is the most natural and readily available substance. K-Y Jelly or any sterile, water-soluble jelly can be used for this purpose. The spermicidal jelly used with a diaphragm is a good lubricant. Vaseline is not recommended, especially if the couple are using a condom for birth control. (Vaseline can cause rubber to disintegrate.)

• *Vaginal infection* can cause sudden stinging or burning during or after intercourse. Sometimes the pain lasts a day or two. The woman usually notes a discharge from the vagina. The three most

---

[2]D. Wilfred Abse, E. M. Nash and L. M. R. Louden, *Marital & Sexual Counseling in Medical Practice* Ed. 2 , Harper & Row, New York, 1974, pp. 234–235.

common causes of vaginal infection are bacteria, yeast (*Candida albicans*) and the protozoan, *Trichomonas vaginalis*. Many things may favor the onset of an infection. A woman is more susceptible during and right after her menstrual period than at other times of the month. Rectal intercourse may introduce germs into the vagina if the husband begins vaginal thrusting without protecting his wife. A woman who has been ill for any reason or who has been taking penicillin, tetracycline or other antibiotics runs the risk of developing a vaginal infection. The discharge from a bacterial infection is usually thick and odiferous. A yeast infection causes a white or cheesy discharge, as well as itching and redness of the skin. Diabetic and pregnant women are more likely to develop a yeast vaginitis. Trichomonas infection causes watery, greenish-yellow discharge that smells bad. Doctors aren't sure how the infection begins, but the germ tends to be passed back and forth from husband to wife. Thus, both partners must be treated for it. Any physician can prescribe the appropriate medication. An infection of the wife's bladder (urinary tract) is yet another cause of painful intercourse. The best way to get relief is to visit a physician and take medicine to clear up the infection.

5. Other Sexual Problems.

The main symptom of a sexual problem is a growing disinterest in sex on the part of one or both partners. Personality problems, financial difficulties, family problems or any other form of discord may be responsible. However, if the cause is sexual dissatisfaction, the first step to solving the problem is a talk with your mate. This may be painful, but it is necessary. The discussion should be tempered with love and understanding. Take a positive approach, and don't blame your mate for failing to meet your needs. Anger and accusations may worsen the problem. Presume that part of the blame is yours, and ask how you can be a more effective sexual partner. If necessary, seek counseling early. Keep an open mind about reaching a solution, and let your love for your mate guide your every action.

Three Sex-Related Complaints and What to Do for Them

1. *"I have a headache"* is something a man may hear his wife say when she has her menstrual period. Her head doesn't ache, but she'd prefer not to give the real reason for wanting to avoid relations. Here's a surprise for you ladies: chances are good that your man would rather know the real reason than an invented one. Smart is the couple who will work out a set of signals that will tell the man ahead of time that his wife is menstruating. A casual, smiling mention that "It's that time again," is all that's necessary. However, the time to make this statement is BEFORE the man gets sexy, not after he's hard and eager.

2. *"Not tonight"* is something the husband (or wife) might hear when the mate isn't in the mood. "No" is a bad word, because it means rejection. Break the rejection cycle by saying, instead, "How about in the morning?". This replaces a negative thought with a positive one. An even better response is for the wife (or husband) to say, "I love you very much. What can I do for you?" The wife might perform oral sex for her husband, or he might stimulate her by cunnilingus or with a vibrator. Here's something to remember: Sometimes the very best sex occurs when one partner is initially reluctant.

3. *"That wasn't too much fun"* is something a man might hear when he had an orgasm but his wife didn't. In the first place, right after sex is not the time to discuss a difficulty. Sex can't be fun when one partner knows that the other is going to criticize the act as if it were a performance. A man who says, "That wasn't too good," puts the same stress on his wife. Chances are that the sex wasn't that great for her, either. Instead of talking it down, talk it up. If you must say something, put a little humor in it. Say, "Well, that one may not make the top ten, but it was still pretty good." After all, every act of intercourse may not be a tumultuous, heart-thumping

one. Sex is naturally better at some times than at others. The nice thing is that the valleys can make the peaks look that much higher.

One Way to Overcome Boredom
in the Sexual Relationship

A man and woman who had been married for ten years developed a unique way of overcoming boredom. The couple had no children, and both held jobs allowing them weekends off. They loved to stay out late on Friday night, and sleep late on Saturday morning. The only problem was that eventually one or both of them had to get up to make breakfast and start the tasks of the day. They hit on the idea of taking turns sleeping in on Saturdays. One weekend the husband would get up and let his wife sleep late, the next Saturday she'd do the same for him. The person who got up served the other breakfast in bed, did the housework, did everything.

One Saturday it occurred to them that they could take turns being "master" and "slave" in their sexual relations. They started immediately, and found the roles very exciting. That particular day the wife could do and get *whatever she wanted*, while the following Saturday her husband got *whatever he wanted*. The arrangement was spicy enough to make them begin taking turns during the week as well as on weekends. The man was able to learn new ways of satisfying his wife, while she learned some techniques that he especially enjoyed. They stopped this practice after several months, but continued to return to it as a cure for boredom in the sexual relationship.

For other ideas on overcoming boredom, refer to Chapters 5 and 6. A special topic for most couples is when—and how—to have sex during and after pregnancy. This is the subject of the next chapter.

8

Sex During and After Pregnancy

Pregnancy is a completely natural event, and one that every couple can be proud of. Some of the happiest moments of marriage occur during pregnancy. The event can bring a husband and wife closer together, and having a child can increase a woman's sexual responsiveness. However, changes occur in the wife's body, and these changes will affect the couple's lovemaking. The purpose of this chapter is to tell about sex during and after pregnancy. Let's begin by looking at the body's reaction to pregnancy.

The Body's Reaction to Pregnancy

Pregnancy lasts nine months, but when you consider that it takes three months for a woman's body to return to normal after birth, you can see that the changes of pregnancy last an entire year. Doctors speak of these as trimesters: three-month intervals. The pregnancy itself consists of three trimesters, and is followed by a three-month period during which the wife's body returns to the way it was before she got pregnant.

First Three Months

A halt in the menstrual periods is usually the first sign of pregnancy, though the period must be at least 10-14 days late to have much meaning. Cessation of the wife's monthlies can be a joyous event when the couple want to have a baby. It can also mean better sexual relations. Pregnancy means that the couple can make love throughout the month, a greater freedom if they usually avoided relations during the menstrual periods. Also, if the wife is indeed pregnant, the couple won't need to use birth control for the rest of the pregnancy. Finally, pregnancy may bring a relief of tension. It proves that the couple can have children if it's the first pregnancy, and it promises a time of joy whether it's the first or the fifth child.

Early in the first trimester the expectant mother's breasts begin to grow. Her nipples may darken, and her breasts may become tender. The tenderness can interfere with the caresses of a husband who is excited by his wife's larger, fuller breasts. A light stroking and kissing of the breasts may be the only stimulation that the wife can tolerate.

Nausea, fatigue and a desire to sleep longer than normal are other changes that may occur during the first trimester of pregnancy. The wife may also discover that she is more emotional than usual.

Second Three Months

The pregnancy creates a rich increase in the amount of estrogen and other secretions which circulate through the mother's blood to support her body during pregnancy. Her amount of vaginal lubrication increases. The couple who've had to use a synthetic lubricant may not need one during pregnancy. This increase in vaginal oils is accompanied by a slight rise in the amount of normal vaginal discharge. The vaginal fluid is clear and not offensive.

Midway during the second three months of pregnancy the mother notes the movements of the baby. At this time, the doctor can hear the baby's heartbeat. The woman's body is becoming larger, and she may have enough appetite to eat for two. She shouldn't. Most of the baby's growth will occur during the third trimester, and late in pregnancy is when most of the mother's weight gain should occur.

Third Three Months

The last trimester is a time of waiting. The woman's body must adapt to the ever-increasing size of her unborn child. She moves more slowly, and walking may become difficult. She may also have trouble with constipation and find that she needs to empty her bladder frequently. This is a time when the wife especially needs the love and support of her husband.

After Delivery

The months after delivery are a time when the wife's body returns to the way it was before pregnancy. Her nipples will gradually lighten. Her breasts will get smaller unless she is nursing the baby. She'll have a vaginal discharge for a couple of weeks after delivery. At first it will look like the menstrual flow, but later it will turn to a clear flow that will dwindle and stop.

It takes two or three weeks for the mouth of the womb to return to the nonpregnant size. Stitches also take this long to heal, and the woman will be sore even if she didn't need stitches. For these reasons, sex is not advisable right after delivery—even though the husband and wife may want it very much. However, the couple can enjoy sexual relations throughout the pregnancy and almost to the time of birth.

Sexual Responsiveness During Pregnancy

Sexual responsiveness during pregnancy depends to some extent on what trimester the mother is in. Let's look at each of these intervals.

● *The first month of pregnancy* is usually no different from any other month, but by the second month the woman notices definite changes in her body. Her interest in sex may heighten, but during a first pregnancy it often lessens. The reasons for this are many. The expectant mother may feel nauseous and find that "morning sickness" may last all day. Nausea and fatigue may daunt her desire for sex. Still another cause for a lessening of interest in sex is a fear that intercourse will harm the developing baby. This fear is groundless.

Judy's Discovery That Her Fear Was Groundless

Judy, a 22-year-old wife who became pregnant, had mild morning sickness and very little fatigue. Even so, she shunned all sexual advances by her husband, Joe. Joe was hurt. Very excited about the pregnancy, he wanted to show his love for his wife. Finally Judy admitted that she was afraid that sex early in pregnancy would harm the baby. She'd heard this from her friends years before, and believed it. Joe insisted that his wife ask her doctor, and Judy did. The physician explained that a woman bothered with frequent miscarriages might have a better chance of a successful pregnancy if she avoided sex during the first trimester. However, this was Judy's first pregnancy, and she was doing fine. She need have no fear of intercourse harming her baby. Judy told her husband, and they enjoyed regular sexual relations until late in the pregnancy. Judy and Joe's child, a girl, was born on schedule and was normal in every way.

Sometimes it's the husband who harbors fears of harming the baby during intercourse. This was true of

The Man Who Needed a Call from the Doctor

In her book *Nine Months, An Intelligent Woman's Guide to Pregnancy*, Alice Fleming described a pregnant woman who became unusually irritable and anxious. The woman couldn't sleep, and had aches and pains throughout her body. Finally her physician, Dr. Flowers, took her aside for a few minutes of confidential talk. The woman quickly admitted that her husband hadn't made love to her since he'd learned that she was pregnant. He treated her as if she were very delicate and very fragile, when what she wanted was his love in a gentle but physical way. The woman asked Dr. Flowers to call her husband and tell him that it was all right to make love to her. The doctor complied, and with the return of lovemaking the wife's aches and pains disappeared.[1]

● *The second trimester* is a time of increasing sexual happiness. A woman's sexual appetite becomes stronger during these months, and she may find that she's more passionate than ever before. She feels better, she's excited about the baby, and she's happy. Her morning sickness is gone, and in its place is a marvelous sense of well-being. This joyous feeling can come as quite a surprise to the wife who's in her first pregnancy.

Betty's Delightful Sexual Experience During Pregnancy

Betty was pregnant for the first time at age 25, and she came in for her six-month checkup all aglow. I thought that she was just in a happy mood, but she had a specific reason for her happiness.

"Is it natural for your sexual appetite to increase during pregnancy?" she asked. I told her that yes, many women found this to be the case. "Doctor," Betty exclaimed, "my appetite is enormous! I think sex night and day. I can't get enough. My husband's the one who can't keep up now. And you know something? Not too long ago we were going to a marriage counselor because I never had orgasms. The counselor gave us some instructions and we've enjoyed sex more, but I'd never had a climax until just a few weeks

---

[1]Alice Fleming, *Nine Months, An Intelligent Woman's Guide to Pregnancy*, Stein and Day, New York, 1972, p. 82.

ago. Now, I have one every time! I'm happier than I've ever been in my life. I think that pregnancy is a wonderful experience!''

● *A woman's desire for sex may stay the same* or diminish during the last three months of pregnancy. During the last month or so, the husband's desire for sex may lessen. The largeness of his wife's body may affect his sexual performance, and so may his unspoken fear of harming her or the baby. Actually, the couple who are aware of a few do's and don'ts need have no fear of enjoying sex during pregnancy.

Six Do's and Don'ts about Sex
Before and After the Baby

It used to be routine for a doctor to advise a woman and her husband not to have sexual relations during the last six weeks of pregnancy and for six weeks after childbirth. This long a period of abstinence is no longer believed necessary. During a woman's orgasm her womb does undergo a brief period of contraction. The squeezing action slows the baby's heartbeat temporarily, but the heart will resume its normal rate within a few seconds. Many women have continued having sexual relations right up until the final day of pregnancy, and had completely normal babies. Sex right after delivery is another matter. The woman may be sore or have stitches, and the mouth of the womb doesn't close completely for some time. It's best, then, to avoid resuming sexual relations until at least three weeks after the baby's birth. Here are the six do's and don'ts:

1. *Do enjoy sex* during the first and second trimesters of pregnancy.
2. *Have sex* during the last three months of pregnancy unless your doctor advises otherwise. He may urge caution if he expects you to have twins or triplets. A multiple birth usually occurs prematurely, and the womb's contractions during orgasm might trigger the premature onset of labor.

3. *Avoid giving* the wife mouth-genital stimulation during the last three months of pregnancy. Air might enter the vagina, be absorbed into the bloodstream, and cause harm. Though an unlikely event, this has happened.
4. *Don't have intercourse* if it causes bleeding or other discomfort. Check with the doctor to see what is the matter.
5. *Don't have intercourse* right after the baby is born. Wait at least three weeks. By this time the woman's vagina is healed and it is safe to have sexual relations.
6. *Do let your doctor* be the final judge in saying how long before delivery you should stop having sex, and how long to wait after childbirth before resuming sexual relations. Incidentally, the mother who chooses to breastfeed her baby may find that it stimulates her sexual appetite. The suckling process itself can be a sensual experience, and may even cause an orgasm. (This is perfectly natural if it happens.) Another benefit of nursing the baby is that it puts off the resumption of the menstrual periods and thus provides some protection against again becoming pregnant. However, breastfeeding alone is not a good means of birth control. See Chapters 13 and 14 for an explanation of ways to avoid pregnancy.

Lovemaking Techniques That Can Give Pleasure Throughout Pregnancy

For the first four or five months of pregnancy, the couple can enjoy intercourse in any position. However, the progressively enlarging womb may interfere with lovemaking in the last months before the child is born. This is when the couple can benefit from special lovemaking techniques (details about each position are given in Chapter 2):

• *The rear entry position* is an excellent one for late in pregnancy. The wife can rest on her side, while the husband does the same and enters her from the rear. This position won't harm the baby and yet will allow mutually enjoyable intercourse.

● *The woman on top position* is excellent during the middle months of pregnancy. By extending her arms, the wife can support her weight and keep her tummy from pressing against her husband's body. Later, when her womb gets larger, she can convert from the woman on top to the sitting position.

● *The sitting position* lets the wife support her body weight and her pregnancy while she enjoys sexual intercourse. The usual sitting position is with the couple face to face. Late in pregnancy the wife may find it more comfortable to sit facing her husband's feet. Intercourse in this position is completely natural, and no cause for a feeling of guilt.

The Couple Who Learned that the Wrong Way Is Sometimes Right

Sue H. became more and more irritable in the last weeks of her pregnancy, and confided to her doctor that she and her husband, Rex, had begun making love in an unusual way. It began one day in the kitchen while Sue was preparing dinner. Her husband was sitting at the table talking to her, and they began to caress. Rex thought it would be exciting to make love right there, and a sitting position with his wife facing away from him was the only position they could manage. Sue enjoyed the lovemaking, but began to feel guilty when Rex insisted on having relations that way every night. Her doctor assured her that this was an excellent position for sex during the late weeks of pregnancy. He also pointed out that the couple could have intercourse in this position in the bedroom in a chair or on the edge of the bed just as easily as they could in the kitchen. Sue accepted the explanation and stopped feeling guilty about a position that, while new to her, was a recommended way to make love during pregnancy.

It is possible, of course, for a woman to satisfy her husband's needs without having intercourse with him. They can assume the rear entry position, and the husband can place his penis between her thighs a few inches above the knees. By clamping down on his penis as he moves back and forth, she can bring him to orgasm. Still another way is for her to stimulate his penis directly.

Joy's Way of Satisfying Her Husband's Needs

Joy W., a 29-year-old mother of three, told me that she and her husband had worked out a way of relieving his sexual tensions during the last weeks of her pregnancy. She stimulated him to orgasm by using the techniques discussed in Step Five of the Sensual Union. She did it without seeking a sexual gift in return. "Listen," she said, "I know of too many husbands who started looking outside the house for satisfaction right about the time a baby was born. I don't ever want that to happen to my husband. And don't worry," she concluded with a wink, "he gets to pay me back after the baby's several weeks old. In fact, he thinks that's the best part of it, because I get more responsive after every baby. I really believe having babies makes a woman enjoy sex more."

A Sensual Union that Improves After the Birth of Children

Interview studies have revealed that for many women sex does get better after birth of the first, second, third and other children. Dr. Mary Jane Sherfey, a leading authority on female sexuality, believes that most women do not reach their full sexual potential until after they've had a couple of children. There are several reasons for this.

First, pregnancy changes forever the woman's sex organs. The vagina and womb enlarge, and the woman has less pain with her menstrual periods. She becomes more relaxed, more at ease with sex. For the first time she may have an orgasm. Her pelvic organs get a better blood supply than before she was pregnant, and this

makes the woman's clitoris and other genital organs more responsive to sexual stimulation. Finally, the woman's husband is apt to
become a better lover. He's a little older, and may go more slowly.
Pregnancy may teach him some things about satisfying his wife's
needs as well as his own. Then too, the presence of a child or
children in the home makes for happiness and a more joyful Sensual
Union.

Sex for the Couple with Growing Children

Children bring something else to the home: a third party and
potential observer of sexual relations. A very young child presents
no problem. By the age of four or five, however, a child can be
inquisitive, intrusive and nosy. Remember that children usually
know far more than adults give them credit for knowing. Seeing his
parents kiss and embrace is healthy for a child, but most couples do
not want their children to see them in intimate relations. Here are
some ways to ensure privacy:

1. *Put a lock on the bedroom door.* Teach the child that at
   certain times, mom and dad need privacy. Arrange for him
   to have something else to do, preferably in his own room.
   Reward him for respecting your privacy, and he'll get the
   message.
2. *Develop alternate places to make love.* Sex after the children are asleep is usually safe, but what if you have a night
   owl teen-ager in the next room? Some suggestions:
   a. *Make love in the closet*—if it's big enough.
   b. *Make love in the bathroom.* A couple of pillows can
      make the tub quite comfortable, or you can have inter-
      course in the standing position in the shower stall.
   c. *Make love on the floor.* Spread a blanket first, or use an
      air mattress for extra comfort. The floor is less noisy than
      the bed, especially if your mattress springs tend to
      squeak.

d. *Make love in the guest bedroom* or in some other room away from the children.

e. *Become conspiratorial* in your attempts to find privacy. Looking for a cozy, private place can be fun. One couple I knew turned the "sex at the office" idea to their benefit. The husband managed a small consulting firm which closed each day at five. Several times a month his wife would drive to the office to meet him after work. As soon as the employees were gone, the couple would retire to a sofa in the lounge and enjoy half an hour of exciting— and uninterrupted—lovemaking.

3. *Send the children to the movie.* A Saturday or Sunday afternoon movie treat for the kids can provide a trysting time for you and your mate. Find out what entertainment is available in your neighborhood, and send the kids to it. Be generous in letting your children out of the house. They'll enjoy getting out, and you'll enjoy the time with your mate!

4. *Go home for lunch.* The man and woman whose children are in school (and who don't teach school) can enjoy an hour of midday privacy by meeting at home for lunch. This is true whether the wife stays home and the husband works, the husband stays home and the wife works, or both work outside the home.

One thing is certain. Every married couple need some time to call their own. In private. Together. A man who previously had all his wife's attention may resent the competition of one or more children. The wife can show him that sharing her love doesn't diminish her affection for him. The husband, by contrast, must realize that his wife will do a much better job of filling her new role as wife *and* mother if she gets his understanding and help. With love and a little luck, the husband and wife will become closer after the birth of children than they were before they began their family.

Still another thing that can strengthen the Sensual Union is to overcome the chronic disease of one of the marital partners. Joyful sex is possible in spite of disease, as we'll see in the next chapter.

9

Joyful Sex
in Spite of
Chronic Disease

Not too many years ago it was taken for granted that a person with a medical condition would have to cut down on sex or give it up completely. Thank goodness this is no longer the case! In most instances you and your mate can enjoy sex in spite of a disease—even if both of you have one. The ways to do this are:

1. *Understand your mate's illness.* You need to know what's wrong with your partner and what physical activities he or she can tolerate. Discuss this with the doctor.
2. *Talk the subject over with your mate.* Talk frankly about the illness, and about the problems it poses. Tell of your continued love, and reassure the person about the future. This gives him or her the valuable knowledge that you are going to continue your life together.
3. *Refer to the Sensual Union* (Chapters 5 and 6), and use these steps to reinvigorate your lovemaking. Give particular attention to Steps Two, Three and Four.
4. *Be aware that sex is a natural body function.* Within certain limits, a healthy sex life can strengthen a person's fight against disease and even improve his mental and physical health.

Sex: A Natural Body Function

Sex *is* a natural function! It stimulates the brain, nerves, muscles, skeleton, genitals, bloodstream, heart and lungs. To some extent it may stress the heart and circulation, but not any more than, say, climbing a flight or two of stairs. Besides, many persons (doctors included) overlook the fact that the victim of chronic disease needs stimulation. Any activity that is fun as well as invigorating can add new meaning to life. Sex can restore the person's pride and feeling of usefulness. It can give something to live for. Consider

The Way Phil Put New Meaning into His Life

Phil C. was a patient of mine who had Hodgkin's disease. This cancer of the lymphatic glands can be relatively mild if caught early, and Phil's chances of living for 10 years or more were good. He didn't care about that. He acted like he'd prefer to die. He seemed overwhelmed by his fever, his fatigue, and his enforced idleness. Things didn't improve after Phil left the hospital and returned home. I saw him every week in the clinic, but just couldn't get him to take an interest in his treatment. Then one day something happened to change that. Phil's wife came with him to the clinic.

Her name was Billie, and she was a shapely, pleasant woman with a bright smile. Standing so that Phil couldn't hear her, she whispered that she wanted to see me in private. We spoke for several minutes while Phil went for a blood test. Billie shared my concern about her husband, and asked if it would hurt for them to resume their sexual relations. She thought sex might be good for Phil. I scolded myself for not having taken the initiative in discussing this important aspect of the patient's treatment. "Of course it won't hurt him," I said, "and it may do him a lot of good. If he has any trouble responding to you at first, just keep trying." She smiled with pleasure and said, "Oh, I don't think he'll have much trouble."

Apparently, Phil didn't. His progress after that clinic visit was nothing less than remarkable. Soon he was able to return to work. With treatment and good luck, he can look forward to years of good life. And his wife can enjoy these years with him.

Four Ways to Enjoy Sex in Spite of Disease

Sex when one or both partners has a chronic illness calls for an extra measure of tenderness and consideration. However, the continuing joys of the Sensual Union are well worth the effort. Here are four ways to enjoy sex in spite of disease:

1. *Don't force sex.* Later in this chapter I'll give the case of Howard, a man who felt that because he'd had a heart attack he had to prove his manhood to his wife. Howard's wife was frightened rather than impressed. Forcing sex is wrong because it takes the fun out of it. Let sex come naturally, when both of you want it. Disease or not, the goal of lovemaking is mutual pleasure!

2. *Begin with a sensuous massage.* Stimulate your mate's body slowly and pleasurably. Focus your attention on non-genital parts first, and then build excitement by stimulating the more erotic areas. One man whose wife had arthritis would begin by massaging her swollen hands and wrists. Then he'd rub her feet and legs. Rubbing led to caressing, and gradually the massage would create the excitement that built up to enjoyable intercourse.

3. *Use the most comfortable position for lovemaking.* Because it is so relaxing, the side-by-side position is the best for intercourse when one partner has a chronic disease. A variant is the rear entry position, where the husband lies behind his wife. The top position is a more strenuous one, and isn't as safe for the person with heart disease. However, the woman on top or the man on top may be the best position to make love when neither person has heart disease.

4. *Learn lovemaking techniques together.* Finding the least strenuous and most pleasurable lovemaking techniques can

be just as much fun when one partner has a disease as when both are healthy. In fact, sex may get better after one mate becomes ill. Sharing and overcoming a problem can be a very stimulating event! At any rate, you can learn to adapt your lovemaking techniques to accommodate for the mate's illness. The rest of this chapter contains a discussion of specific diseases and how to enjoy sex in spite of them.

Sex for the Person with Heart Disease

Heart and vascular disease is so common that almost half the people in this country can expect to die from it. On the other hand, treatment for heart disease is better than ever. The victim can survive for years and years. He can and should enjoy sexual relations.

The Risk

Sex stimulates all of a person's vital signs. During orgasm, his heart rate, breathing rate and blood pressure may double. This puts a strain on the heart, and the victim of heart disease runs the risk of sudden death during intercourse. However, such deaths are uncommon. A curious fact is that a man with heart disease is much more likely to die during intercourse with another woman than during relations with his wife. Perhaps his anxiety about the affair is more stressful than the sex itself. Not every man who collapsed during a sexual climax knew beforehand that he had heart disease, so it may be that the person who does know his limitations is lucky. He can build himself up to withstand the physical demands of coitus.

The Body's Ability to Cope

You wouldn't start out to run a mile without first training for the task, and the same is true of sexual intercourse after a heart attack. First, the damaged heart muscle needs time to heal and strengthen itself. The body is able to cope, but the heart patient must wait, walk, and watch his weight:

- *Wait* as long as your doctor tells you to wait before becoming physically active. This means no sex or other strenuous activity until you get the go-ahead.
- *Walk* under your doctor's guidance. The modern trend is to encourage walking fairly soon after a heart attack. Movement strengthens the heart and helps to prevent clots from forming in the legs. By six weeks after your attack, you will probably be able to walk 15 minutes at a time. Gradually, you can go further. How far and how fast you eventually go will depend on your heart function and on how much effort you put into your exercise program. In the book *Heart Attack? Counterattack!*, Dr. Terry Kavanagh of the Toronto Rehabilitation Center tells of men who have survived a heart attack and gone on to run in the Boston Marathon.[1]
- *Watching the weight* helps the heart by reducing the work that it must perform. Walking and other forms of exertion (including sex!) help you to lose weight, but a diet may also be necessary. A complete discussion of ways to prevent or treat heart disease is given in Chapter 5 of my book, *A Medical Doctor's Guide to Youth, Health, and Longevity*.[2]

The Rules to Follow

When you reach the point of being able to walk at a brisk pace for 30 minutes, you've recovered sufficiently from your heart attack to withstand the strain of sexual intercourse. This degree of physical conditioning will usually occur somewhere between *two and three*

---

[1]Terence Kavanagh, *Heart Attack? Counterattack!*, Van Nostrand Reinhold, New York, 1976.
[2]John Deaton, *A Medical Doctor's Guide to Youth, Health and Longevity*, Parker Publishing Company, Inc., West Nyack, New York 10994, 1977.

months after the heart attack. It may take longer if your attack was severe, or not so long if it wasn't. Check with your doctor, and if you're ready for intercourse, here are some rules to follow:

- *Have sex in a relaxed*, comfortable setting. Don't let the room be too hot or too cold.
- *Don't have sex* right after a meal. The heart is busy with digestion, and intercourse will put a greater strain on it.
- *Use the side-by-side position*, or let the person with heart disease take the bottom position. This keeps exertion to a minimum.
- *Don't have sex* when you've been having chest pain, shortness of breath or a lot of swelling of the feet and legs.
- *Keep nitroglycerin tablets* nearby and use them if you get chest pain during intercourse. It's not a good idea for a man to take nitroglycerin *before* intercourse, because the drug might keep him from having or maintaining an erection.
- *Remember that these rules* apply equally to the woman who has heart disease. During intercourse, her heart is put under the same stress as a man's.

Something to Avoid

A heart attack can be as destructive to a man's ego as it is to his heart. The thing to avoid is an overreaction, a foolhardy attempt to prove yourself to your wife.

How Howard Reacted the Wrong Way to His Heart Attack

Howard got out of the hospital three weeks after his heart attack, and insisted that he and his wife resume their sexual relations immediately. They did, though Howard's wife wasn't sure that her husband was up to the strain of intercourse. Elizabeth was a nurse, and knew something about the limitations imposed by a heart attack.

She was also surprised when Howard insisted on having sex every night; their previous frequency had been about once a week. Elizabeth decided to discuss the problem with Howard's doctor.

The physician said that Howard's reaction wasn't all that unusual. "A man who's had a heart attack may feel he's lost his manhood," the doctor explained, "and having sex with his wife may be the only way for him to prove to himself that he hasn't." Elizabeth admitted that Howard had begun to question her about her enjoyment of sex. This was something he had not done before. "My suggestion," the doctor continued, "would be to reassure him that you love him and think he's every bit the man he used to be. At his next visit I'll see if I can work the subject around to sex and tell him to take it easy for three more weeks."

Howard and Elizabeth soon settled into their normal frequency of relations, but Howard was lucky. His need to prove himself could have cost him an unnecessary strain on his heart and another heart attack.

Other Kinds of Heart Disease

The person with a heart murmur may or may not need to restrict his activities. In most cases the murmur has been present a long time and the person is adjusted to it. He can and should enjoy sex. A very severe heart murmur is a different matter. It may place a strain on the body and limit the person's ability to engage in sexual intercourse. In fact, the first evidence of heart strain may appear during coitus.

Helen's "Lifesaving" Collapse
During Sexual Intercourse

Helen T., a 19-year-old woman, collapsed while having intercourse with her husband, Tommy. They'd been married only two weeks, and Helen had noticed that she became short of breath each time they had relations. However, on this occasion she blacked out from a lack of oxygen. Tommy rushed her to the hospital, where doctors treated her for *pulmonary edema*—a dangerous condition of heart failure and waterlogging of the lungs. When Helen could breathe more easily, she was admitted to the hospital for a complete workup.

Studies showed that her heart had been damaged by a childhood attack of rheumatic fever. The disease, mitral stenosis, had grown progressively worse. Helen had a loud heart murmur, and the strain of intercourse had caused her to go into heart failure. The heart specialist told her that the collapse might just have saved her life. It brought her to the hospital where she could be treated in time to prevent a fatal heart failure.

We gave Helen digitalis and other treatment. A few months later, a surgeon replaced the damaged valve in her heart. She recovered completely, and was able to resume all the activities of married life. Helen subsequently became pregnant and after an uneventful pregnancy gave birth to a healthy boy.

Sex After a Stroke

A stroke occurs when part of the brain is deprived of its blood supply. A clot in a blood vessel can cause it, and so can rupture of a vessel in the brain. The victim develops paralysis of one or both sides of his body, and other problems such as slurred speech. Fortunately, these changes are usually reversible. The person can expect to recover partial or total use of his body, and even during his recovery he can resume a normal sex life.

Desire for Sex

A 1967 study showed that 60% of stroke victims either had the same desire for sex as before the stroke, or wanted sex even more frequently than before the illness. Even so, 40% of the persons had intercourse less frequently than before the stroke. In some instances loss of body function was the cause. In other cases, the marital partner was reluctant to initiate sex. Don't be! An illness that distorts the body can strike a devastating blow to a person's self-esteem. The love and intimacy of the marriage partner can work wonders in speeding the stroke victim's recuperation!

Ways to Enjoy Sex

When to resume sexual relations after a stroke is a question for the doctor to decide. An important factor in the decision is whether or not the person's blood pressure is under control. Medicine can control an elevated pressure, but adjusting the dosage takes time. As a rule, sex is safe beginning a week or so after the stroke victim gets home from the hospital. Here are some guidelines to follow:

1. *The paralyzed person* has to tell his partner what feels good and what doesn't. Paralysis is usually limited to one side of the body (most commonly, the left side). The skin on this side may feel "dead," or it may be exquisitely tender. Moreover, the sensations tend to change as the person improves. For this reason, the stroke patient should take the lead in showing his partner what forms of stimulation are most effective.
2. *The best position for intercourse* depends on the site of paralysis and on the position that is most comfortable. A person with a paralyzed left side, for example, may prefer to lie on his right side during intercourse. He can use pillows to prop himself in this position. It may help to put a handle on the headboard of the bed. By grasping it, the stroke victim can move about more freely in bed. Still another idea is to put a footboard at the free end of the bed for better support. These items can be purchased at a medical supply store or built by a good craftsman.
3. *Lubricant* in the form of water-soluble jelly or spermicidal jelly will make intercourse easier when a woman stroke victim can't produce sufficient lubrication of her own.

4. *Use the Techniques Discussed in Step Five of the Sensual Union* to help a male stroke victim overcome impotence (in the event that he develops this problem). Most of the time the stroke is not the cause of impotence. The problem may be a depression, medicines the man is taking, or excessive use of alcohol. Steps Five and Eight of the Sensual Union can be used to generate feminine ardor when the wife is the stroke victim.

5. *A problem with bladder control* can be overcome by emptying the bladder before having sex. This will prevent an accident during lovemaking. The man who has a catheter in his bladder can learn to remove and reinsert it, or his wife can learn this technique (under a doctor's or a nurse's guidance).

High Blood Pressure

High blood pressure can usually be controlled by drugs, salt restriction and a regular exercise program. The person need not limit his sex life. Severe high blood pressure can cause heart disease, kidney disease or stroke. Still, even severe high blood pressure can usually be controlled by drugs. Don't hesitate during one of your check-ups to ask the doctor how much exertion and sexual activity you can tolerate. Then, follow his advice. You may need to lose weight and get started on a regular exercise program; when you can walk briskly for twenty or thirty minutes a day, you can tolerate sexual intercourse. However, you should probably limit the frequency of intercourse to no more often than once a day.

Lung Disease

Sex for the person with lung disease is perfectly all right so long as it doesn't cause undue shortness of breath. One way to minimize the strain on the lungs is to have intercourse in the sitting position. A patient of mine with severe lung failure had to sleep sitting up. Every hour of every day he wore a green nasal catheter that carried oxygen from a portable tank to his nose. And yet this man not only enjoyed sex, it perked him up and gave him something to live for. Probably the most important things a person with lung disease can do are to stop smoking and to lose weight. These measures will improve his health as well as his enjoyment of sex.

Asthma

Asthma is an allergic condition that causes the person to have attacks of wheezing and shortness of breath. Good treatment of the asthma will usually allow the person to have a normal sex life. The treatment includes taking desensitization treatment, bronchodilators and a drug called cromolyn sodium, which helps to prevent asthma attacks. It's a curious fact that an emotional upset can trigger an attack of asthma. In fact, sexual arousal has been known to set off wheezing and shortness of breath in a susceptible person.

The Man Who Breathed Hard
at the Wrong Time

Alfred had been a victim of asthma since childhood, but he and his wife had enjoyed normal sexual relations until after the birth of their first child. Then, Alfred began to have wheezing attacks whenever he and his wife, Martha, began to prepare for intercourse. The problem grew so disturbing that Alfred visited a psychiatrist.

The psychiatrist learned that as a child, Alfred had been punished severely for masturbating. His mother had an uncanny knack for catching him at it, and Alfred's defense was to have an asthma attack. Ever since then, Alfred had begun wheezing when he felt threatened. Questioning revealed that he now felt that Martha was a threat to him. Since the birth of their baby, Martha had become bossy and much more demanding. Subconsciously, she had become a mother figure to Alfred. Their attempts at sex reminded him of punishment at the hands of his mother, and thus provoked his wheezing.

The physician brought Martha into the treatment program. When she understood the cause of Alfred's asthma attacks, she became less demanding of him. His wheezing stopped and they were able to resume their sexual relations.

Diabetes

Mild diabetes doesn't interfere with a person's sex life. In fact, the weight loss that is usually a part of the treatment can improve sexual performance. Diabetes can be controlled by insulin and diet, but when it gets out of control, problems are bound to occur. Sometimes, even a minor difficulty can seem like a major one.

The Day Gale Visited Her Doctor for Relief

Gale had been on insulin for years, but hadn't been taking good care of herself. She and George, her husband, had gotten in the habit of eating irregularly. Her diabetes got out of control, and this became apparent one night during attempted intercourse. Because Gale's genital area was raw, George's attempts to insert his penis were quite painful to her.

Gale learned from her doctor that she had a severe infection of the vagina. The infection, caused by the yeast *Candida albicans* (monilia), is apt to occur in a diabetic woman who spills sugar into her urine. Treatment of the condition gave Gale prompt relief, but she and George had to avoid intercourse for a week until the infection was completely eradicated. The doctor also readjusted Gale's insulin dosage and put her on a diet that would keep her diabetes under control. By taking good care of herself, Gale had no further problem with the vaginal infection.

Infection is not the only possible complication of diabetes. The person who's had diabetes for a long time may develop a problem with the nerve sensation to various body parts (though not usually the sex organs). Good treatment may prevent this complication, so the best thing for the diabetic to do is to take his medicine, follow the prescribed diet, go in for regular check-ups, and notify the physician when a problem arises.

Arthritis

The victim of arthritis can usually continue to enjoy the same pleasures he has always enjoyed. This includes a normal, fulfilling sex life. Here are three tips that will add to the person's sexual pleasure:

1. *Have intercourse in a comfortable position.* The arthritic's hands may be stiff, so it stands to reason that he should avoid supporting his weight on them during intercourse. The same goes for stiff or painful elbows, shoulders and knees. The side-to-side position is a comfortable one for intercourse, or the arthritic may prefer to take the bottom position.

2. *Enjoy a warm bath before having sex.* Nothing provides quicker, better relief for stiff joints than a nice warm bath. Add some perfumed bubble bath to the water and make it a sensuous scrub. The greater mobility of your joints after the bath will enable you to be a better lover.

3. *Take your arthritis medicine in the evenings.* Make it your habit to save one dose of your medicine for the evenings, if that's when you choose to have sex. Take this dose before you get into the warm tub, and it will have time to start acting by the time you finish your bath. Taking medicine before sex is an excellent way for an arthritic to get more pleasure out of sex, but this tip wouldn't have appeared here if I hadn't discovered

Joyce's Way of Enjoying Sex
Despite Arthritis

Joyce, a woman in her early thirties who had rheumatoid arthritis, told me that she and her husband had almost given up sex in the first months of her illness. The movements of intercourse were painful to her back, but one day she discovered something. She was on a small dose of a cortisone drug, and was supposed to take it each morning. One day she forgot the dose until late afternoon, and was amazed at how much better she felt that evening. She and her husband made love, and next morning Joyce called to say how happy she was. She wanted to know if it was all right to take her medicine in the evenings instead of the mornings. We compromised by having her take half the dose in the morning to overcome early stiffness and the other half in the evening for the time with her family. Next visit, Joyce reported that she and her husband were enjoying a better sex life than they had in months. She made me promise to pass along to all my patients her discovery of how a small change in the way a patient takes her medicine can mean a big difference in her marital happiness!

Liver and Intestinal Disease

The person with a mild liver or intestinal disorder can continue to have sex as often as he wishes. When his abdomen is sore or swollen, he may prefer to have coitus in the sitting position. Oral-genital stimulation as described in Step Five of the Sensual Union is an alternate way of providing sexual gratification.

Ulcer is a common affliction of middle-aged men, and the treatment is for the person to recognize that there's more to life than work and stress. An improved Sensual Union is not only fun, it's therapeutic! Go on a vacation, relax, and enjoy each step of the Sensual Union (Chapters 5 and 6).

Drugs That Can Lower Sexual Desire

Certain drugs can reduce a person's sex drive. Among these are:

- *Blood pressure pills*—including methyldopa, reserpine, hydralazine, spironolactone and guanethidine.
- *Tranquilizers*—including diazepam, meprobamate and chlordiazepoxide, which are prescribed to relieve nervousness.
- *Sleeping pills*—such as barbituates and flurazepam.
- *Pain medicine*—such as morphine, codeine, meperidine and oxycodone.
- *Ulcer pills*—atropine, propantheline bromide and other drugs that reduce stomach acidity.
- *Antidepressants*—including the tricyclics and other drugs used to treat depression.
- *Stimulants*—such as amphetamine, methylphenidate and ephedrine.
- *Cortisone preparations*—such as prednisone, cortisone and hydrocortisone.
- *Hormone treatment*—such as the use of estrogen to treat a man with heart disease or cancer of the prostate. Estrogen is the female sex hormone and the man who takes it may lose his sex drive.

Your doctor would not prescribe one of these drugs unless he thought you needed it. On the other hand, you may outgrow that need, or prefer to have your sex drive back at any cost. Discuss the problem with your physician, and he'll be able to help you.

Cancer

Many cancer patients can be cured, and others can take medicine or other treatments that will prolong life for years. Good sex is possible—and desirable. A Sensual Union makes life for the cancer patient more enjoyable, and is especially meaningful to the marriage partner. I'm reminded of

The Man Who Enjoyed Good Sex
until the End

Jack C. got lung cancer when he was in his early fifties, and by the time it was diagnosed the cancer was too far advanced for a surgical cure. Doctors gave Jack x-ray treatments. I saw him each week in the clinic, and was amazed at how well he coped with his illness. In fact, he seemed to radiate a sense of inner contentment and happiness. One day as he was leaving the office he said, "Doc, you're going to think this is funny, and maybe I oughtn't to say it, but sometimes I think my life didn't start till I found out I had cancer. Janet and I have never been so close as we are now."

Jack lived for two more years. After his death, his wife thanked me for my help. I expressed my admiration for the way Jack had found happiness in spite of his cancer. Janet said that she, too, had been amazed at her husband. "He told me he didn't know whether he was going to live for one year or two years or how long, but that during what time he had he was going to live life to its fullest. He began by going back and treating me as if I were still his high school sweetheart. Our sex life improved, everything improved. Doctor, I wouldn't take anything for these last two years, because they're the most precious of my life."

Cancer can destroy a part of the body, and the surgeon may have to remove the tumor as well as the surrounding normal tissue. This can change the person's appearance, but the important thing is that it won't change him. The couple can continue their sex life. Here are some specific conditions and suggestions:

• *Lung cancer.* Removal of all or part of a lung may be necessary. Surgery leaves a scar, but the person can usually breathe and move normally. If sight of the scar is bothersome, the person can wear a tee shirt or undergarment to keep it covered during sexual relations.

• *Breast cancer.* Removal of a breast may be necessary to treat breast cancer. The extent of the operation may vary, but one thing holds true for every mastectomy patient. The woman can wear a specially fitted artificial breast that is as soft (or firm) as normal flesh. She can keep her bra on during sex, and her husband will hardly notice the difference. Or, the couple may prefer to remove all clothing and make love to each other as before. More than one patient has told me that sex got better after a mastectomy. "It made us appreciate each other more," is the way one woman put it.

● *Cancer of the prostate.* The prostate is a plum-sized gland that sits beneath a man's bladder; cancer that occurs in it can be treated by medicine, surgery, or both. Removal of the prostate will change a man's volume of ejaculate, and the cancer medicine such as estrogen hormone may lower his desire for sex. Even so, he can usually continue to have sexual relations. If impotence becomes a problem, the man should check with his physician or refer to the information given in Chapter 7.

● *Cancer of the rectum or colon.* After removing a cancer of the bowel, the surgeon may perform a colostomy—an operation to create a colon opening through the front wall of the abdomen. This allows the person to digest food normally, but waste material enters the colostomy bag for disposal instead of passing on to the rectum. Since the colostomy bag collects waste, its presence might seem like an unsexy barrier to lovemaking. To coin a phrase, love conquers all! The couple can enjoy sex in spite of the collecting bag. For one thing, you can't hurt the colostomy by hugging or embracing, and for another, you can hide it from view by wrapping a clean towel or pillow case around it. The woman whose husband has a colostomy can take the top position for lovemaking, but she might prefer the bottom position if she is the cancer patient. The rear entry position is another way they might choose to have intercourse.

Skin Disease

Nine out of ten skin rashes aren't contagious, so you need not fear catching anything from a partner with skin disease. Many skin conditions are mild and intermittent, and don't interfere with sex. Certain diseases are more chronic. Psoriasis is an example. The scaly, raised rash makes its appearance on the head, elbows, knees and scalp. No cure is known, but many medicines can help to control it. Most treatments require the rubbing of an ointment or salve onto the rash. The marriage partner can apply the treatment as part of a sensuous massage or a prelude to sexual relations.

Excess growth of body hair may be a troublesome problem for a woman. Birth-control pills can stimulate hair growth, so as a first step you might try switching to another form of contraception. The drug Dilantin, which is taken to control epileptic seizures, may cause undue hairiness. The person may be able to switch to an anticonvulsant that doesn't cause this problem. A skin specialist can remove unwanted hair, but the treatment is time-consuming and expensive. Perhaps an easier way for a woman to solve the problem is to bleach the hair so that it won't show. Be careful not to harm your skin during the bleaching process.

Acne follows some persons into adulthood. Pimples and black-heads can distract from one's appearance, and these skin blemishes can lower a person's opinion of himself. In the first place, masturbation is NOT the cause of acne. Neither is too much sex or too little sex. Acne is caused by staph bacteria that grow on the skin. All people harbor these bacteria, but most persons develop a resistance to them that prevents acne. The person with problem acne should see a doctor. The physician can prescribe an antibiotic such as tetracycline, antibiotic ointment for use on the skin, and soaps and lotions that will keep the skin clean and dry. By taking birth control pills, a woman may be able to rid herself of acne.

A disease shouldn't stop you from enjoying the sexual side of marriage, and neither should the passage of years. Sexual happiness during middle age and later years is the subject of the next chapter.

10

Sexual Happiness During Middle Age and Later Years

With good health and a willing partner, you can continue to enjoy sex throughout middle age and the later years of life. The ways to do this are to:

1. *Remember that sexual enjoyment for the married couple can and should continue throughout life.* Forget what you may have heard about sex sizzling out beyond a certain age. Aging does not take away the sex drive of a normal person.
2. *Understand that a woman's desire for sex continues at a high level after her menopause.* Her response to sexual stimulation may be slower than that of a younger woman, but she is still capable of excitement, orgasm and sexual satisfaction.
3. *Realize that beyond the age of 50 or 55, a man may have a slower response to sexual stimulation.* This is perfectly normal, and doesn't mean that he is unable to have an erection or to enjoy sexual intercourse.
4. *Draw on your years of experience in lovemaking to continue your Sensual Union.* Put your expertise to use! If anything, the Sensual Union should get better with the passage of time.

How Sex Can Get Better with the Passage of Time

Maybe youth *is* wasted on the young. Certainly a mature person has the perspective to enjoy and appreciate the sexual relationship more than he did when he was younger. Maturity, after all, is a time for relaxation and joy. Family and financial responsibilities are fewer. There's more time for travel and entertainment. But the middle-aged or older person has other reasons to continue to enjoy sex.

A woman's sex drive tends to increase in her thirties and forties, and remains as strong as ever right on up into her sixties, seventies and beyond. A man's desire for sex may decline slightly as he enters his fifties and sixties, but his performance may improve. He's less apt to demand an ejaculation with every act of intercourse, and thus he may become a better lover. Indeed, many couples enjoy a second honeymoon in their early fifties—a honeymoon that continues for years and years. The beginning of this period of enhanced sexual pleasure may coincide with the woman's menopause.

Lovemaking During and After the Menopause

Menopause is the date of the last menstrual period (the word means "cessation of the monthlies"). A woman will experience this between the ages of about 45 and 55. However, for a year or so before the menopause she may have irregular menstrual bleeding, hot flashes and feelings of discomfort. She can and should continue to enjoy sex during these years, but some women have difficulty doing so. This is a time for tenderness and understanding on the part of the husband. The wife needs his support and love.

Wilma's Discovery That Sex Can Get Better After the Menopause

Wilma had her menopause at age 50. She and her husband, Robert, had enjoyed sex regularly since their marriage 30 years previously. They'd raised a family and now lived alone in a large house on a street with many other couples their age. Soon after she began to have hot flashes and irregular menstrual periods at the age of 49, Wilma noted pain during and after intercourse. The problem persisted and she visited a doctor. He could find nothing wrong with her. Wilma was angered by this, because she knew there had to be a reason for her pain and discomfort. She was nervous, too, and her frustration reached the bursting point that evening when her husband got home from work.

She told him she'd been depressed for several months, and that she knew that in another year or two she'd be old and undesirable. Robert would probably leave her, or find himself a younger woman. "But it doesn't matter," she said, "because our sex life is over! You keep wanting it no matter how I feel, but you can just forget it! You can leave me if you want, but that's the way it's going to be. I'm old and I'm ugly and I'm finished!"

Robert, who shared this episode with me, said that he'd suspected his wife's symptoms were related to her change of life. He took her in his arms and told her that she was more beautiful than ever to him, and that he didn't want to be away from her even if they never had sex again. Robert's support touched Wilma. She cried herself to sleep that night, but felt happier the next day than she had felt in years. Soon she and Robert began to make love again. Wilma still felt slight pain, but got relief from an estrogen cream her doctor prescribed. She and Robert overcame the temporary inconvenience of menopause, and their lovemaking became more passionate and enjoyable than it had been years earlier.

The Physical Changes of Menopause

Menopause occurs because the woman has reached the age when her ovaries no longer make the same quantities of sex hormones they did previously. After her menstrual periods stop, she's no longer capable of becoming pregnant. Her body undergoes other changes. Those that most affect her sexual responsiveness occur in the pelvis. Three things happen to the vagina:

1. Its walls become thinner.
2. It releases less oil during intercourse.
3. Vaginal lubrication occurs more slowly than previously.

These changes don't begin right after the menopause. The wife whose menstrual periods stop at age 55 may not notice any change in vaginal lubrication or in the thickness of her vagina until she is 60. This means that a woman going through the menopause has no physical reason not to continue to enjoy a Sensual Union with her husband. Beyond the age of about 60 she may note the vaginal changes just mentioned, but these need not keep her from enjoying sex.

Four Ways to Ensure That a Woman Can Have Sexual Happiness at Any Age

With a little attention to her body and to lovemaking techniques, a woman can continue to be sexually responsive in spite of the menopausal changes that occur in her body. Here are four ways to do this:

1. Stay sexy!
2. Develop a Sensual Union.
3. Use a lubricant if necessary.
4. Take estrogen therapy if it is indicated.

1. Stay Sexy!

Masters and Johnson found that an active sex life tends to keep a woman's vagina working efficiently and healthily well beyond the age of menopause. According to these researchers, three women past the age of 60 showed an effective vaginal response to sexual intercourse. These women had something in common. Each person had continued to enjoy an active sex life throughout her reproductive years and afterwards. On the other hand, a woman beyond the age of 55 or 60 who stops having regular sexual relations is more likely to have trouble on the rare occasion that she attempts to have intercourse. It's as if the vagina, like any body part, will continue to work efficiently so long as it is used regularly. The wife who stays sexy assures herself of a continuing and satisfying Sensual Union.

The Woman Time Forgot

Libby H. was a 72-year-old woman I helped to care for during her hospitalization for surgery. The amazing thing about Libby was her age, or rather, that she looked at least fifteen years younger than she was. Her husband was 55 (it was the second marriage for both), and he took pride in his wife's youthfulness. "She doesn't get older, she gets better," he said, and meant it. The physician who performed Libby's hysterectomy (necessary because of a benign tumor of the uterus) said that his patient's vagina lacked most of the postmenopausal changes one would expect at her age. "Her condition is amazing," he said. "It's mighty rare to see a woman in her late sixties who's as well-preserved as Libby."

The patient recovered from her surgery quickly and left the hospital. I've always regretted not asking her the reason for her youthfulness, but there was no reason to ask. I could sense that she and her husband enjoyed a Sensual Union. Libby's body was living proof that staying sexy is not only enjoyable but youth-giving.

2. Develop a Sensual Union.

The Sensual Union program was given in Chapters 5 and 6. One of the nice things about the two-week training period is that a couple is never too old to start it. Particularly important is Step Three: the exploring of the mate's body for new ways to build sexual excitement. A woman beyond the age of menopause may need more physical stimulation from her husband to reach a peak of sexual excitement. For one thing, her vagina is more sluggish in releasing the oils that provide the lubrication for intercourse. By working through Step Three together, the couple can discover ways of making foreplay both exciting and effective.

It's not a bad idea, in fact, for every couple to rejuvenate their Sensual Union at about the time of the wife's menopause. Doing so may come quite naturally when the wife realizes that she no longer has to worry about getting pregnant and that she can relax and enjoy sex more freely than ever before.

The Couple Who Went on a Second Honeymoon

Dianne and Tony R. were a couple my wife and I met at a resort on the Colorado River near Austin. They were both 51, and it was easy to tell that they were delightfully, refreshingly in love. I thought they were newlyweds, and said so one night at dinner.

"Well, we are on a honeymoon," Dianne told me with a laugh, "but it's our second. We've been married thirty-two years, and loved every minute of it. But you know something? I've just been through the change, and I'm a liberated woman! Things have never been so good between us."

Tony agreed. "You two just wait," he said, "and you'll see what she means. You'll discover that your second honeymoon is much better than the first."

There's no reason why you and your mate can't enjoy a second honeymoon to celebrate the menopause. It's a time to develop new and sensuous lovemaking techniques and to enjoy sex for the sheer delight of the experience. If life begins at forty, the Sensual Union may not begin in earnest until the husband and wife are in their fifties!

3. Use a Lubricant if Necessary.

A young woman tends to develop vaginal lubrication within 15-30 seconds of the onset of sexual stimulation. A woman beyond the age of menopause may require 4 or 5 minutes of sex play before her vagina is moist enough to permit comfortable intercourse. Usually, a slow and sensual lovemaking technique will allow the wife's natural secretions to flow. If necessary, however, use a synthetic lubricant. You may choose K-Y Jelly, Lubifax or any water-soluble jelly, or you may prefer to use a body oil. The lubricant can be applied to the mouth of the vagina or to the penis. In fact, applying it can be an intimate and enjoyable part of foreplay. The husband can oil his wife's vagina and stimulate her mons and clitoris with a delicate massaging motion. In turn, the wife can apply lubricant to the husband's penis. The application of lubricant can be a pleasant ending to a sensuous massage.

4. Take Estrogen Therapy if it Is Indicated.

Estrogen is one of the hormones produced by a woman's ovaries, and the lesser amounts of it that are produced after menopause are what cause the vagina to become thinner and to release less oil. The lack of estrogen may be responsible for pain occurring during intercourse. The pain may be felt at the start of intercourse, or persist as an ache or burning in the vagina or surrounding region for a day or so after intercourse. Thinning of the vagina is the usual cause, and estrogen therapy may correct the problem.

How Florence Got Over
Her Pelvic Pain

I had seen Florence W. several times for a blood pressure condition before she told me that she had another problem. "It's my husband," she said. "He keeps wanting to have relations. I don't mind, but it's got to where it gives me pain. I wish you'd talk to him." Florence was 74, and her husband was 76.

An examination showed that my patient's vagina was thin from a lack of estrogen, and that she had a mild irritation in it. I prescribed an estrogen-containing cream to be applied to the vagina several times a week. At a subsequent visit, Florence reported that she no longer had pain during intercourse.

Physicians are not in full agreement on the indications for estrogen therapy after the menopause. Estrogen-containing cream is an accepted treatment for thinning or dryness of the vagina, because very little of the hormone is absorbed into the bloodstream. Still, some women who use the cream will develop soreness of the breasts. The soreness tends to leave after the medicine has been used for a month or two. The use of estrogen tablets such as Premarin is much more likely to cause side effects.

At one time, drug companies promoted estrogen tablets for every woman past the age of menopause. The woman's ovary no longer makes enough estrogen, the argument went, so why not replace the "deficiency" with synthetic estrogen? The problem is that estrogen therapy does more than just replace a "deficiency." The hormone may favor the growth of a tumor in the breast or uterus, promote the formation of blood clots in the woman's vessels, or cause other side effects. Still, the woman whose estrogen lack keeps her from enjoying sex may want to take the risk. A medical exam will show whether estrogen might help, and should uncover any reasons for not taking it. It's necessary to get regular medical check-ups during therapy with estrogen tablets or estrogen-containing cream.

Lovemaking by the Middle-Aged or Older Man

A normal man doesn't go through the same type of menopausal symptoms as does his wife. In fact, the man's testicles may continue to make testosterone and sperm cells for all of his life. This is why men in their eighties or older have fathered children, and it's why an older man who can't achieve an erection won't necessarily improve when given testosterone injections. His sexual function does change, however, as a man gets older. In his forties he may not notice any change from when he was in his twenties and thirties, but beyond the age of 50 he may have less sex drive and more trouble achieving an erection.

The Golden Years of a Man's Life

In general, five things happen to a man's sexual responsiveness as he gets older:

1. *He notes less interest in sex than he used to have.* He may not desire intercourse quite so frequently.
2. *He responds more slowly to sexual stimulation.* It may take several minutes of sex play for him to develop an erection.
3. *He feels less urge to have an ejaculation with every episode of intercourse.* For example, he may be satisfied to ejaculate every second or third time he has coitus.
4. *After ejaculation, his erection leaves more quickly than was true when he was a younger man.*
5. *He may not be able to have another erection for 12-24 hours after he has ejaculated.*

These changes are perfectly natural, and may work to the husband's advantage. Gone are the hot passions of youth, and in their place are the experience and skill of a mature lover. Since he has less urge to ejaculate, the mature man's erection tends to last longer. He's better able to enjoy the pleasure of lovemaking—and to stimulate his wife fully. This means that even though the frequency of sexual relations may go down, the *quality* of the Sensual Union generally improves. In addition, the man and his wife can take advantage of six ways to ensure their continuing sexual happiness:

Six Ways to Bring the
Golden Years Man
Rising to Action

1. Stay sexy!
2. Mingle sex with quiet and relaxation.
3. Avoid overuse of alcohol.
4. Let praise speak loudest.
5. Put variety into lovemaking.
6. Use the best technique of sexual arousal.

1. Stay Sexy!

Masters and Johnson found that men who remain sexually active during middle age and later years are less likely to have performance problems than are men who go without sex for long periods of time and then attempt to resume sexual relations. In other words, the happily married man should have no difficulty enjoying a Sensual Union well into his seventies, eighties and beyond. The message is clear. Good sex is healthy, and the couple who enjoy good sexual relations will continue to do so in spite of age.

However, the man who notes difficulty achieving an erection may benefit from the techniques listed below.

2. Mingle Sex with Quiet and Relaxation.

Sex and stress don't mix! A man in his forties, fifties or sixties may have risen to a place of responsibility in his career. The phone rings constantly, each day brings a new crisis that must be managed. All this is distracting, and the best strategy may be for the couple to get away from the house every week or two. Some couples enjoy going to a mountain retreat, a seashore, a river—whatever happens to be appealing and available. I know of one couple who lock their house and tell everyone they're leaving town, but don't! They just pretend they're in a motel, and it works for them.

3. Avoid Overuse of Alcohol.

As he gets older, a man's sexual performance is more vulnerable to interference from a drug such as alcohol. Let me tell you about Guy's problem and the way he conquered it.

Guy's Discovery of a Way
to Increase His Sexual Performance

Guy, a successful banker in his early sixties, came in for his yearly check-up. After I'd examined him, I told him that he was in good health and asked if he had any questions. Guy hesitated, and then said that his sexual performance was not what it should be. A moderate user of alcohol, he had two drinks before dinner, and one or more afterwards. He was surprised to learn that alcohol could blunt his sexual response. "I thought it was the other way around. That's why I've been drinking even more on the nights that my wife and I plan to have sex. But from what you tell me, I should drink less." He followed my suggestion to avoid alcohol when he planned to have sex. It worked.

By depressing brain function, alcohol can keep even a young man from achieving an erection. An older individual is especially susceptible to its influence. Thus, avoiding alcohol before sex is a way of improving one's sexual performance.

4. Let Praise Speak Loudest.

A man's body may grow older, but chances are very good that in his heart he still considers himself a virile youth of sixteen. How he feels about himself means everything in his ability to have an erection. Therefore, the wife should never tease him or put him down when he's slow at achieving a full sexual response. The danger of teasing him is that the man may begin to think that he has a problem. He does not—though worry and fear may create one. It's much wiser for the wife to praise her husband. Tell him that it doesn't matter, and that just being with him is enough to make you happy.

5. Put Variety into Lovemaking.

The man's problem may be boredom, and this is where Sensual Union training can help. Go through Step Three again, and learn new ways to build sexual excitement. Try new things together (Step Four), and dress up your Sensual Union as sexily as possible (Step Seven). Do things differently, and you'll enjoy better sexual relations!

6. Use the Best Technique of Sexual Arousal.

A man enjoys a sensuous massage and general stimulation of his body, but the best way for his wife to arouse him is by sucking his penis (See Step Five of the Sensual Union). This simple and loving technique may help the man to achieve an erection when all else fails.

How to Add Sparks
to a 40-Year Marriage

Jess and Maurene O. had been married for 40 years before they had any sexual difficulties. Then, Jess had trouble achieving an erection. After a time or two of failure, he stopped trying. Maurene was disappointed, because she still wanted to enjoy sex with her husband. Earlier in their marriage he'd wanted her to give him mouth-genital stimulation, but she wouldn't. She remembered this and decided to try the technique. It worked. After several minutes, Jess achieved a full erection. He and Maurene had better sexual relations than they'd had in years. To Jess the technique meant a new and exciting form of sensual pleasure, and to Maurene it meant the difference in her being able to have intercourse with her husband. The surprising thing to Jess was that once Maurene had reawakened his interest in sex, he no longer needed mouth-genital stimulation to achieve an erection. Maurene's willingness to love him in this special way was all the stimulation he needed to regain his sexual vigor.

The Unique Thing about Sexual Responsiveness After Age 60

I've known many couples like Jess and Maurene. They grew older thinking that sex would soon die out, but it didn't. Instead, they discovered that sexual love can be a source of lasting joy. The unique thing about sexual responsiveness after age 60 is its importance to the individual. The sexually happy couple can expect to live longer and to live better than would otherwise be the case.

How do you and your mate remain sexually happy into your golden years? You do it by getting all the pleasure you can out of each of your sexual experiences. Continue your Sensual Union a day at a time, and the future will take care of itself! If there's any secret to sexual happiness in the golden years, it may be that such couples know how to enjoy better sex at any age.

Five Ways to Enjoy Better Sex at Any Age

1. *Love one another, and tell of your love.*
2. *Show your love in the way you respect your mate and do things for him or her.* Be courteous, tender and understanding.

3. *Do things together.* Spend time alone together every day, and never grow too old to try new things.
4. *Develop a joyful and lasting Sensual Union.*
5. *Give yourself special care just for your mate.* Sexual happiness grows out of your own self-esteem, which means that you should dress and care for your body in a way that is most likely to give you and your mate sexual happiness. Things a woman can do to have sexual happiness are the subject of Chapter 11, and the things a man can do to have sexual happiness are the subject of Chapter 12.

11

Ten Ways a Woman Can Increase Her Sexual Responsiveness

Sexual happiness comes so easily to some couples that they're scarcely aware of the ingredients that go into it. Effort, of course, is necessary. The wife must do her part, and the husband must do his. The plain fact is that the more one puts into the sexual relationship, the more one can expect to get out of it. The purpose of this chapter is to show ten ways that a wife can heighten her sexual responsiveness, and the next chapter will treat the same subject for the husband.

How Every Wife Can Become a Sensuous Woman

Being a sensuous woman doesn't mean that a wife has to spend hours at the beauty parlor each day, hours soaking in a tub, and still other hours preparing a sexy nest for her husband. She may prefer to do her own hair, take a shower, and hire someone to clean the house! The important thing is what she feels about herself and her husband. She may be a housewife, have a career in addition to her marriage, or be retired, but one thing every wife has in common is that she is the key to the Sensual Union. Her husband's desire for her, coupled with her desire for him, is what makes sex a source of continuing excitement. By making herself more appealing to him and by improving her intimate performance, the wife can increase her own sexual happiness. The ten ways to do this are:

1. *Heighten your body magic in three special ways.*
2. *Use tried and proven feminine methods.*
3. *Trim down and tone up.*
4. *Do the intimate exercises that will please him—and you!*
5. *Take advantage of a special treatment if necessary.*
6. *Be as sexy as your husband wants you to be.*
7. *Wear the right thing for the right occasion.*
8. *Master the feminine art of undressing.*
9. *Generate your own fervor.*
10. *Discover the perfect aphrodisiac.*

#1: Heighten Your Body Magic in Three Special Ways.

Sex goes far beyond the physical, of course, but the magic begins when the husband and wife kiss, caress and become intimate. Three ways to heighten your body magic are to be squeaky clean before sex, to keep your skin smooth and lovely, and to wear just the right perfume.

● *Be squeaky clean before sex.* Many women prefer a long hot bath before sex, while others prefer to take a quick, invigorating shower. Still others manage to stay squeaky clean with a morning bath and a late afternoon or evening swim. The wife should do what works best for her. Cleansing of the vulva is especially important, because secretions can gather there. Too, the sweat glands in this part of the body have strong secretions that may produce a characteristic odor. Most men prefer a natural, clean smell. Washing with a mild soap and lots of water is the sexy, natural way to bring out your body magic. Some couples enjoy bathing together, and begin their sex play in the tub or shower.

The Couple Who Started Sparks
Flying in the Shower

Dora and John, a couple in their twenties, reported that they began showering together on their honeymoon, and had enjoyed the practice ever since. They liked the body contact, the shared wetness, and the way they had to yell at each other above the roar of the spray. What they enjoyed most, though, was getting to wash one another.

"We didn't do that at first," John said, "but it didn't take long to start it. I began by washing her back and she washed mine. Then one thing led to another."

Dora and John found it stimulating and sensual to wash one another's genitals. For them, this was a variation of Step Three of the Sensual Union. They began by washing and caressing the nongenital areas, then moved on to the more sensitive parts. Each partner got a chance to explore their mate's body and to discover ways of giving sexual pleasure. The sexual excitement that started in the shower carried over to mutually satisfying intercourse afterwards. Sometimes Dora and John would have relations in the bathroom, but they usually preferred to continue the lovemaking session warm and dry in the comfort of their bed.

● *Keep your skin smooth and lovely.* A woman's sex hormones cause her to have a soft padding of fat beneath her skin. This cushion is both provocative and useful. It is important to a woman's sex appeal, and it represents stored energy for use during pregnancy or nursing a baby. Do your best to keep your skin and its padding as attractive as possible. Removing unsightly hair comes first. Shave the legs and under the arms once or twice a week—more often if necessary. Most women don't shave above the knees, and removing the pubic hair is certainly not a good idea. It's all right to trim it, though, if you wish. Removing hair from the underarms and legs will please the husband in two ways. He'll enjoy the sight of you better, and your skin will be smooth and less likely to prickle him during lovemaking.

Skin blemishes may require special treatment. The bumps of acne can appear on the face of a fully grown woman—especially one with an oily complexion. The simplest treatment is to wash the face thoroughly with soap and water four times a day. You don't need a washcloth. Your fingers can work the lather in gently and effectively. About once a day, apply a mild drying agent to your face after it's clean. A liquid drying agent containing 5% benzoyl peroxide is best. Select one in the skin care department of a pharmacy. (You don't need a prescription for it.) The drying agent may cause slight chapping of your face, but the idea is to reduce oiliness and thus cut down on the amount of acne. However, if your skin becomes too dry, stop using the drying agent or use it only once a week. Don't eat chocolate, nuts, cola drinks, French fries, sharp cheeses and other spicy or greasy foods. Acne care is more difficult when the bumps appear on the back, chest or hips. Probably the best strategy for a woman with problem acne is to visit a skin specialist (dermatologist). Among the treatments he can offer are antibiotic therapy, dietary tips, special cleansing lotions and instructions on the use of a sun lamp or ultraviolet light to remove the bumps.

Even one bump in the wrong place can interfere with sexual activity. Let me tell you about

The Five-Minute Treatment that Revitalized Betty and Oscar's Sensual Union

Betty didn't have acne, but she had developed a small skin cyst on her right groin. She hardly noticed the peanut-sized swelling, but her husband did notice it. Oscar stopped wanting to kiss or caress his wife's genitals. In fact, sight of the swelling tended to kill his interest in sex. Betty, while trying to decide what might be wrong, discovered the bump during her bath. She came in to have it removed, and the treatment took only five minutes. On the way out she explained her reason for wanting it removed, and promised that she'd give us a follow-up. She called the nurse a few days later to report that relations between her and her husband were "revitalized."

● *Wear just the right perfume.* Just the right perfume may be no perfume at all, or it may be a scent you've worn for years and that you know will excite your husband. One scent you do not need is that provided by a "feminine hygiene spray." In fact, these products may harm you by causing an allergic reaction. Save your money. Cleanliness and maybe a little scented body powder are much more enticing.

#2. Use Tried and Proven Feminine Methods.

The vagina has a natural cleansing action of its own. Occasionally a drop or two of clear fluid may stain the panties (it may turn yellow on exposure to the air), but throughout most of the month the vagina will have no discharge or bleeding. The times when care may be necessary are after the menstrual period and after having sexual relations. The best care is a properly administered douche.

Three Tips in Using a Time-Honored Treatment

The three tips in using this time-honored treatment are to douche only when necessary, to use the right solution, and to give it the right way:
● *Douche only when necessary.* The times when you may want to douche are after a menstrual period and after having sexual relations. Not every woman desires to douche after her period, but if it makes you feel cleaner, do so. Douching after intercourse is another matter. If you use a vaginal foam for contraception, or a jelly and diaphragm, you shouldn't douche right after having sex. You might wash the contraceptive material away. Postpone douching for at

least eight hours after having intercourse if you use a vaginal product for birth control (see Chapter 13 for a discussion of birth-control methods). A woman who takes the Pill or who doesn't have to worry about getting pregnant may prefer to douche to remove semen from the vagina. It's easier to wipe the semen out, but douching will remove it also. The wife who wants to get pregnant, of course, should leave the semen in the vagina. For that matter, douching is not a reliable method of birth control.

● *Use the right solution.* Douche solutions can be bought in the drugstore, but you're better off using a home remedy that also happens to be the douching solution most often ordered by doctors when a patient in the hospital needs this treatment. The solution is a mildly acidic one. You make it up by mixing two tablespoons (one ounce, or 30 cc) of white vinegar to a quart (1000 cc) of water. To make twice this amount, you'd add two ounces of vinegar to two quarts of water. Normally, one quart is sufficient for one douche.

● *Give it the right way.* Douching is a method of cleansing the vagina. For it to work, it must be done in the right way. The best place for the procedure is in the bathroom with you on your back in the tub. (It's very difficult for a woman to give herself an effective douche while sitting on the toilet bowl.) The douching equipment consists of a container for the solution and a rubber or plastic tubing that is connected to the container. At the far end of the tubing is a douche tip, and just above it is a shut-off clamp. Once the solution is in the container and you've taken your position in the tub, insert the douche nozzle halfway into the vagina. Then, by positioning the container on the bathtub rim and releasing the clamp, you can allow the water to flow into the vagina. Rotate the nozzle gently during the douche so that the solution will reach all parts of the vagina. Remove the nozzle when the container is empty. You can dry yourself off afterwards, or you may prefer to take a bath when the douche is completed.

Three Precautions

Douching too frequently can cause problems. It may irritate the vagina and cause a discharge. It's best to douche only when necessary and as infrequently as possible. Three precautions about douching are:

1. *Don't use a douche during pregnancy.* The danger is that it might cause an infection in the womb.
2. *Don't use a douche for six weeks after pregnancy.* Once again, the douche might cause an infection of the womb.
3. *Don't use a douche solution other than water and vinegar except as prescribed by a doctor.* The mixture of water and vinegar imitates your natural secretions. Other solutions may irritate the vagina.

#3. Trim Down and Tone Up.

One of the sexiest things an overweight wife can do is to lose weight! The weight reduction will improve her looks as well as her sexual performance.

Jackie's Discovery of a Way to Rekindle Her Husband's Interest

Jackie had been overweight for 10 years. Until she and her husband were in their thirties, however, their sex life had been satisfactory. Then Bob, Jackie's husband, seemed to lose interest in her. His loss of interest occurred at a time when Jackie suddenly seemed to put on a lot of weight. It was as if her sexual frustration caused her to eat more, which compounded the problem. My suggestion to Jackie was that she first try to stop gaining weight, and then see about losing it. Exercise proved very helpful to her, and she took up tennis, bike riding, and walking. As the months passed she managed to lose 20 pounds and to tone up her body by using her muscles. She and her husband resumed their sexual relations, and that was all the encouragement Jackie needed to continue her weight reduction program.

Good Health and Happiness Go Together

There's no escaping the fact that healthy people are happy people. Health implies a normal body weight, and reducing will prolong your life and give you more enjoyment and satisfaction every day that you live. You can lose weight in three ways: (1) By going on a diet to take in fewer calories than you normally burn; (2) By exercising to burn more calories than usual; or (3) By combining diet and exercise to lose weight more quickly. You can get details on losing weight in my book, *A Medical Doctor's Guide to Youth, Health, and Longevity*.[1] The important thing to realize is that good health and sexual happiness do go together. Begin today to trim down and tone up!

#4. Do the Intimate Exercises That Will Please Him— and You!

The vagina is a pouch that extends several inches into the pelvis. Near the vulva it is surrounded by muscles that form a girdle to hold the pelvic contents in place and assist the woman in starting and stopping her stream of urine. The main muscle is the pubococcygeus ("PC" for short). It can be weakened during childbirth, and a woman who's had several children may notice that because of the weakness she loses a small amount of urine when she coughs, sneezes or strains. Surgery can be done to correct this problem, but Dr. Arnold Kegel of the University of Southern California School of Medicine developed a series of muscle exercises that women can use to strengthen a sagging PC muscle. These exercises can do more than control the involuntary loss of urine. By doing them a woman can enhance her sexual pleasure and that of her husband.

---

[1]John Deaton, *A Medical Doctor's Guide to Youth, Health and Longevity*, Parker Publishing Company, Inc., West Nyack, New York, 1977.

The Delightful Discovery Made
by Dr. Kegel's Patient

The first patient Dr. Kegel asked to do these exercises was a woman with three children who complained of accidentally passing urine when she'd laugh or cough. She followed the exercises, got relief from her urine problem, and made a discovery. For the first time in fifteen years of marriage, she had an orgasm during intercourse. She told the doctor about this, and he duly noted the observation in her case record. Before long, other women who had performed the exercises were confiding the same thing to Dr. Kegel. Along with the correction of the urinary difficulty came an unexpected enhancement of sexual pleasure. A cause-and-effect relationship seemed apparent.

How the Exercises Increase Sexual Pleasure

At first, Dr. Kegel wasn't sure how strengthening the PC muscle could enhance a woman's sexual pleasure. His studies had shown that the PC muscle was like a sling that surrounded and supported the vagina, and that a woman with a weak PC muscle tended to have loose, sagging vaginal walls. The exercises changed this. The woman's vaginal muscles got stronger and she was better able to feel the pressure of her husband's penis during intercourse. This created more stimulation of the sensitive nerves in the walls of the vagina and increased her sexual pleasure.

Surprisingly, the husband also began to enjoy sex more. A woman's PC muscles go into reflex tightenings at the moment of her orgasm and exert a squeezing action on the penis. This greatly enhances a man's sexual pleasure.

Who Can Benefit from the Exercises

Not every woman has weak vaginal muscles. A wife who hasn't had children, for instance, is less likely to have a weakened

PC muscle than is the mother of four or more children. On the other hand, the strength of the PC muscle doesn't correlate with bodily strength. A woman athlete may have a weak PC muscle, while a secretary who does nothing more strenuous than peck a typewriter may have a strong PC muscle. Three groups of women who can benefit from doing Kegel's exercises are:

1. *Women who've had children.*
2. *Women who've noticed the involuntary loss of urine during a laugh, cough or sneeze.*
3. *Women who don't reach an orgasm during sexual intercourse.*

By examining you, a gynecologist can tell whether you have PC weakness and might benefit from doing the exercises. One thing to bear in mind, however, is that doing the exercises won't hurt you. Thus, you can try them out and see if they work for you.

How to Do the Exercises

Step One. The most important step in doing Kegel's exercises is to learn to recognize which muscle is the PC muscle. Once you've learned to contract it, you can do the exercises almost anywhere. To locate the muscle, sit on the commode with your knees widely separated. Begin to pass urine. Then, interrupt the flow of urine. To stop your urine stream you must tighten your PC muscle. Repeat this maneuver several times until you're certain you recognize the feel of a tightened PC muscle. You can check to see if you're contracting the right muscle by positioning yourself on your back on the bed. Spread your knees and use a mirror to watch the region between your vagina and anus during a PC contraction. The region should lift or tighten when you contract your PC muscle. The feeling is similar to the sensation you may get when you need to pass urine but must hold it until a more convenient time.

Step Two. Begin doing the PC tightenings about six times a day. Each tightening takes only a second or so, and the exercise needn't be limited to when you're in the bathroom. You can contract the PC muscle while standing in a grocery line, sitting on a sofa watching TV, or while resting in bed the first thing in the morning after you wake up. During the first week of exercising, try to do ten tightenings in a row. This is a total of 10 x 6, or 60 contractions of the PC muscle a day.

Step Three. After one or two weeks, you'll be ready to increase the amount of exercise. Begin doing 15 contractions six times a day for a total of 90 a day. The third week, go to 20 contractions six times a day—a total of 120 a day. Your eventual goal is to do 30 contractions at a time, six or seven times a day (a daily total of about 200 PC contractions). After about two months of the exercises, your vaginal muscles should be strong and you should notice an improvement in your sexual responsiveness. After reaching this point, you needn't continue doing so many tightenings. About 100 contractions a day done once or twice a week should keep the PC muscle strong. However, after having a baby you'll have to start back at Step Two to rebuild the strength of the muscle.

Sexual Benefits

Use your PC muscle to exert a firm, sensuous pressure on your husband's penis during intercourse. The timing of the squeezing actions are up to you. One good time is during or just after entry of the penis into the vagina. The husband will also like the tightening as he nears orgasm. Probably the best idea is to try contracting the PC muscle at various times during intercourse. Then, settle on the technique that gives you and your husband the most pleasure.

#5. Take Advantage of a Special Treatment if Necessary.

Some women with weak PC muscles do not wish to do Kegel's exercises, or they find that the exercises offer little benefit for them. These persons may need surgery to tighten the walls of the vagina. The operation, known as an ''anterior and posterior vaginal repair,'' or "A-P repair," can be done by a general surgeon or gynecologist. In most instances, it will heighten a woman's sexual responsiveness. Sometimes an A-P repair is done in combination with a vaginal hysterectomy, the removal of the womb from below by making a cut in the upper part of the vagina. Hysterectomy may become necessary when a woman has a growth in the uterus or is bothered by heavy menstrual bleeding that cannot be controlled with drug therapy. By having a muscle tightening done at the time of hysterectomy, the woman can get relief from involuntary loss of urine. She may also discover that the surgery enables her to get more pleasure out of sexual relations.

#6. Be as Sexy as Your Husband Wants You to Be.

The best way for you to increase your sexual responsiveness may be to focus on giving your husband what he likes. Be as sexy as he wants you to be! Do your part to develop each step in the Sensual Union, and you'll enjoy it as much as he does. Seduce him for a change; replace "no" with "yes!"; develop new positions and techniques of lovemaking. In other words, let yourself go!

Earlier in this book I spoke of how leaving the lights on during lovemaking would add to a man's enjoyment of sex. But you needn't leave the lights on every time. Make love in the dark if it suits you better. Show by your uninhibited behavior that turning the lights off can be as exciting as leaving them on!

#7. Wear the Right Thing for the Right Occasion.

Step Seven of the Sensual Union tells about wearing sexy costumes to arouse your husband. Increase your own responsiveness by dressing right for a sexy occasion. Planning the event can be exciting, and the sexy surprise may result in very pleasurable intercourse.

One thing you might try is wearing a cat suit or anything with pointed ears. The sight of pointed ears is enough to bring out the animal in any man! This is one secret that explains the sexiness of the Playboy Bunny; those long, floppy ears do it. Make your suit a bunny suit if you like, or try a pitch-black cat suit. Just have long pointed ears on the cap, and spring the costume on your husband when he's in the mood. Go all the way and purr a few times and say "Meow!" as you pad around the bedroom. He'll get the message.

Sexy nylons or bikini underwear may excite your husband. Maybe he'd prefer you in a sheer negligee. Arouse him in the most erotic costume you can think of, and you'll be the one who benefits the most!

#8. Master the Feminine Art of Undressing.

Just as important as what you wear is how you take it off. Many wives are surprised to learn that the sight of a partially clad body may be more sexy to the husband than full nudity. The key to generating sexual arousal in undressing is to reveal a little at a time, but not too much at once.

How Susan Learned to Excite
Her Husband Throughout the Evening

Susan, an attractive blond, said that very early in her marriage she'd found that by arousing her husband she aroused herself. She went about the arousal in stages throughout the evening. She wore soft things to show that she was in a sexy mood, and would change into a jersey or silk dressing gown when she got home from work. The gown gave her a graceful allure as she prepared dinner, and made her a sexy partner for kissing or caressing during the evening. Before her bath she'd remove the gown, making sure that her husband got a glimpse of her shoulders or legs. She'd reappear in a half slip or shortie nightgown to do those feminine things a woman does before bathing, and after the bath she'd slip into the sheerest of negligees. By this time of evening her husband was fully aroused and ready for passionate lovemaking. And so was Susan.

Undressing, like other forms of sexual play, benefits from variety. Surprise your husband with a view of your breasts or thighs. Or, go into the closet fully dressed and come out a moment later wearing nothing. The blunt quick beauty of his wife's nude body is bound to please any husband. He may prefer a slower, more seductive undressing, but he'll love being surprised now and then.

#9. Generate Your Own Fervor.

The wife who doesn't enjoy sexual relations is said to be "frigid," though the meaning of this word is changing. For one thing, frigidity is not a once and always condition. A wife's failure to enjoy sex may reflect her husband's lack of skill as a lover. Moreover, the wife may want sex at some times but not at others.

Problems of Frigidity

Frigidity becomes a problem when the wife no longer wants to go on trying to enjoy sexual relations. Sexual intercourse may hurt, or lovemaking may be a frustrating ritual. Her loss of interest in sex naturally frustrates her husband, and creates marital difficulties. Divorce is frequently the outcome.

The thing the couple should realize is that a solution can be worked out. No woman is sexually unresponsive! If she loves her husband and wants to enjoy sex with him, she can do so.

How to Generate Your Own Fervor

The causes and some solutions for frigidity were discussed in Chapter Seven under the heading "The Woman Who Doesn't Reach a Climax." One point that bears repeating is that the woman who can bring herself to orgasm through self-stimulation is more likely to have a climax during sexual intercourse. The reason for this is that masturbation will teach you about your own sexual responsiveness. It will help you to generate your own fervor.

Choose a private part of the house at a time when you're not likely to be interrupted. Undress and relax. Now may be a good time to view your body in the mirror and get acquainted with its unique features. Work yourself into a sexy mood by thinking about your husband and the kind of satisfying sexual relationship you'd like to have with him. Take your breasts in your hands, explore your stomach and hips and thighs. Stimulate your clitoris and main lips lightly with your fingers. Rubbing the mons or adjacent parts will also provide clitoral stimulation. Do what feels best. Some women prefer light stimulation at first, progressing to more vigorous rubbing of the clitoris. You may want to stimulate your clitoris with one hand, your breasts with the other. Or you may prefer to use a vibrator instead of your hands and fingers. One very stimulating technique is to get in the tub and let warm faucet water splash directly on the vulva (you may need a spray nozzle attached to the faucet). In fact, there's nothing to keep you from experimenting with several techniques in one session. Whatever method you choose, you may not reach a climax, at least at first. Let your goal be enjoyment. In time you will reach an orgasm. Then, you can show your husband how to excite you, and help him to incorporate these techniques into his lovemaking.

How Delores Overcame Her Unresponsiveness

Delores W. was married for the second time and still did not enjoy sex. Her physician suggested she try self-stimulation to generate her own fervor, but Delores refused. She had been raised to believe that any form of self-stimulation was wrong. The doctor hinted that Delores might get the same benefit by having her husband, George, do the stimulating for her. Delores agreed to try.

Step Three of the Sensual Union taught Delores and George several new ways of stimulating one another, but they carried it a step further. When Delores was sufficiently excited, George would place his hand over her vulva. Then, Delores would move his fingers to stimulate herself in any way that felt good. George, of course, cooperated. After several sessions, Delores became so excited that she reached a climax. George caressed her for a few minutes more, then gently initiated intercourse. Delores had another orgasm, and it coincided perfectly with George's. Their shared pleasure made Delores and George very happy. They were even more thrilled by Delores' discovery that she was a very sexually responsive woman.

#10. Discover the Perfect Aphrodisiac.

An aphrodisiac is something that increases sexual desire and enjoyment. Some people think that Spanish fly (cantharides) is one such substance, though it doesn't really increase sexual desire. In fact, Spanish fly may be very harmful to the body. Amyl nitrite, a drug used by some persons with heart disease, can increase the intensity of orgasm if it is inhaled during intercourse. A woman who takes the male sex hormone, testosterone, will usually have a greater sex drive, but the hormone might cause her to grow whiskers and develop an enlargement of the clitoris. Drugs such as alcohol, marijuana and opium are as likely to depress sexual desire as to increase it.

The only perfect aphrodisiac is one you may not have thought of—to love your husband. Sexual desire grows out of his love for you and your love for him. Love is the only aphrodisiac you need, and it happens to be the perfect one!

12

Ten Ways a Man
Can Increase His
Sexual Responsiveness

*M*any couples automatically assume that the husband is more sexually responsive than the wife. This isn't necessarily the case. He may be less desirous of sex than his wife, or he may fail to provide her the stimulation she needs when they do have intercourse. One thing is clear. The husband's sexual responsiveness encompasses not only his desire for intercourse but his ability to fully satisfy his wife. The purpose of this chapter is to show how a man can increase his sexual responsiveness.

How Every Husband Can Become a Sensuous Man

It's possible for a husband to be the most sensuous man in the world for his wife. He can do this by fulfilling his role as her lover. Love, after all, is what binds the married couple together. Satisfying sexual relations help that love to grow and deepen. By becoming a better lover, the husband stands to make his wife happier and to increase his own sexual enjoyment. The ten ways to do this are:

1. *Achieve the look, feel and scent of love.*
2. *Be the "he-man" you can be!*

3. *Keep a clear head for greater ardor.*
4. *Enlist your wife's aid in those "special" moments.*
5. *Let your natural urges be your guide.*
6. *Sacrifice pride for pleasure.*
7. *Discover the joy of slow, sensual lovemaking.*
8. *Use your "second" sex organ to elicit passion.*
9. *Share your sexual turn-ons with your wife.*
10. *Discover the secret of sexual attractiveness.*

#1. Achieve the Look, Feel and Scent of Love.

The way to achieve the look, feel and scent of love is to be yourself—with a little polish. You are the one your wife loves, and your body is attractive to her. Enhance your sensuality by adding the right smell and feel to your masculine features.

A Love Potion Available to Every Man

It's true that the smell of her husband's perspiration may turn a wife on. However, he shouldn't always count on this. That nice, clean, post-shower smell is likely to be just as enhancing, or more so. Water is a love potion, because by cleansing your skin it makes you smell just the way you used to smell when you went to court her. She associates that smell with love and romance. Practice preparing for sex in the same way you used to dress for a date.

Brush your teeth thoroughly, and brush your tongue. Use dental floss several times a week, and brush again after flossing. Use mouthwash if you wish. Make sure your hair is clean and appealing. Top off your preparations with your favorite deodorant, cologne or after shave.

Smell is a powerful sexual stimulant, so here's another tip. Select one brand of cologne or after shave that you and your wife like, and stick with it. Let her come to associate this fragrance with your presence. Then, in those close-up moments of sex play, she can catch the scent of love. Remember that you don't have to splash on a handful of the stuff. Just use a little on your face and neck.

Shaving itself can be mighty important (unless you are a bearded husband). Most men shave in the morning, but a husband may discover that by evening his growth of whiskers makes him less than appealing to his wife.

The Man Who Protected
His Wife's Skin
and Made Himself Sexier, Too!

Virgil K. got up early each morning, shaved, and left for his job with a pipe company. By the time he returned in the late afternoon he had a heavy growth of beard. For the first several years of their marriage, Virgil and his wife, Sally, had enjoyable sex despite the whiskers. Then one morning Sally awoke to find that she'd developed a rash on her face. The "rash" turned out to be whisker burns, and Sally tactfully suggested that maybe her husband ought to shave twice: once in the morning and again in the evening. Virgil was more than happy to do this; he simply hadn't realized that his whiskers hurt his wife's face. An added benefit was that his smooth face made him more appealing to his wife. Their sexual relations improved when he began shaving and grooming himself each evening before supper.

How often you need to shave depends on your growth of beard. I've known men who could shave every other day and still have a smooth face, and others who had to shave two or three times a day to stay presentable. If you insist on shaving just once a day, the best idea may be to do it in the evening before dinner.

Some men are bothered by acne and oily skin. If you're one of them, you can benefit from using the same methods of face care that I gave in the preceding chapter. Wash your face thoroughly in the morning after shaving, and get in one or two good face scrubs during the day. You needn't carry a bar of special soap in your pocket. Stash it in the restroom where you work, or use the bar or liquid soap that is supplied. Wash again when you get home from work, and again at bedtime. Apply the drying agent the last thing at night or right after your morning toilet.

#2. Be the "He-Man" You Can Be!

As he grows older, a man looking into a mirror tends to see that same youthful, virile fellow that he has always seen. His wife and others may see him differently. Obesity is a very common condition in the United States, and it becomes more common as one gets older. A "pot," "spare tire," or general tubbiness can occur so slowly that you hardly notice it. Have one? If so, remember that it may affect your health as well as your sex appeal. Be the "he-man" you can be by reducing to your ideal weight based on your height and frame size. You can get tips on weight reduction in my book, *A Medical Doctor's Guide to Youth, Health, and Longevity*. I recommend the trimming down and toning up approach. This is a combination of diet and exercise to lose weight, and it is something that a husband and wife can do together. In fact, a daily walk or jog together is one of the sexiest habits that a married couple can cultivate.

The Couple Who Practiced a Sexy Habit Together

Margie and Don A. were in their early sixties, yet both were as trim and attractive as they had been since they were in their thirties. They enjoyed good health and a happy marriage. Don came in for a routine office visit, and during the course of my admiring his physical health, I asked him for his secret. His wife answered my question.

"Exercise!" she said. "He's been doing it since before we got married. In fact, our dates used to be for him to come get me and me to go watch him play ball. Then after we got married, I told him that I wanted to be more than a spectator. I happened to enjoy activity myself."

"That's when we hit on the idea of a daily walk together," said Don. "We go out every day after supper, and after lunch on a weekend. I think walking together is a wonderful habit for a couple. It gives us a chance to talk to each other and to share what we've done during the day. I don't know why, but it's gotten to be such a meaningful part of our lives that I don't think we could do without it."

Almost every couple can benefit from Margie's and Don's advice. The exercise may be golf, tennis, biking, swimming, jogging or walking. The man who takes the trouble to keep in shape will have better health and a better sex life. Thin, he's more attractive to his wife and apt to be a better lover. What's more, the good health he enjoys by being physically fit will enable him to savor the pleasure of sexual relations more fully than would be the case if he were out of shape.

#3. Keep a Clear Head for Greater Ardor.

Sexual arousal tends to occur more quickly in a man than in a woman. Even so, a man's erection is the result of a complex interaction between the circulatory and nervous systems. Many things can hinder a man's ability to have an erection. Among these are drugs such as alcohol, tranquilizers, sleeping pills and blood pressure pills.

Many men mistakenly believe that alcohol elevates sexual responsiveness. A small quantity of alcohol may lower a man's inhibitions and make him more desirous of sex, but the drug will reduce his performance. It can prevent him from having an erection, or from sustaining an erection that does occur. Tranquilizers, sleeping pills and some of the drugs used to treat high blood pressure can have the same effect. One other action of these drugs is to cloud a man's thinking so that he may be less considerate of his wife's feelings and less able to give her the stimulation she needs to reach orgasm.

It just makes sense for a man to keep a clear head during lovemaking. Refraining from alcohol or limiting his intake of it will make him a better lover and will increase his and his wife's sexual pleasure. The same can be said for sleeping pills and other drugs. If you believe that a prescription drug is taking the edge off your sex drive, ask your doctor to prescribe a different drug. Or, possibly, you may be able to take the drug in the mornings instead of the evenings. If you must take the drug twice a day, make the evening dose the last thing you do before going to sleep.

#4. Enlist Your Wife's Aid in Those "Special" Moments.

Failure to have an erection is something that will happen on occasion to just about every man. This is no cause for embarrassment. It is, instead, a challenge that the husband and wife can meet together. One of the sweetest things the wife can do is to show her husband that she doesn't need to have intercourse to be completely happy with him. This relieves him of the pressure of having to perform. Still another way she can be of help is to stimulate the penis. She might begin by giving her husband a sensuous massage and gradually focusing her attention on the penis. She can move the foreskin up and down over the glans, or take the penis into her mouth and suck it or nibble on it or stimulate it with her tongue.

The husband shouldn't remain passive. He can give his wife a sensuous massage, and caress the parts of her body that she enjoys having massaged. His erection may occur while he is caught up in her reaction to clitoral stimulation, or while he is fondling and kissing her breasts.

#5. Let Your Natural Urges Be Your Guide.

A man's desire for sex isn't as constant as his appetite for food. For a week or two he may want sex every night or several times a day. Then, his level of passion may fall. He may prefer to have intercourse once a week, or be satisfied with sex every other week. Things that happen to him during the day may influence his sexual desire (or lack of desire). The important thing is that he realize that upswings and downswings of sexual desire are perfectly normal. Let your natural urges be your guide, and learn to concentrate on quality rather than quantity.

The Couple Who Found That Less Can Be More

Sam and Sarah, like many newlyweds, thought that sex was something they would enjoy every night for the rest of their lives. After several months of marriage, however, they began to tire of nightly intercourse. Sam was actually glad that his job required him to leave town for a week. At night in the hotel room, he thought about Sarah. He bought a paperback novel and enjoyed reading the sexually explicit passages. He found himself planning the things he and Sarah would do when he got home.

Sam's homecoming was a joyful one. He introduced mouth-genital contact into their lovemaking, and he and Sarah began to have intercourse twice a day. Good as the sex was, the couple found that they couldn't keep up this pace. Sam mentioned this to his wife, and was surprised to learn that she, too, was more desirous of sex at some times than at others.

"We made an agreement right then," Sam said. "We decided we'd have sex when we wanted it, and not just because we thought we were supposed to. What we did was cut down on the quantity and increase the quality. And if we keep discovering new things together, I don't see any end to the fun we can have."

Sam and Sarah had discovered that good sex is enjoyable sex, no matter what the frequency. Good sex is more apt to occur when both partners are in the mood. The special chemistry of marriage occurs when the husband can sense that his wife is in the mood and can match his own mood to hers.

#6. Sacrifice Pride for Pleasure.

It's no exaggeration to say that American men are more competitive than any other group of men in the world. They work hard, play hard and strive to reach the top. This striving for the top may work to a man's disadvantage in his sexual relations. His wife may get more pleasure out of making love in the woman on top position, and he should let her. It may hurt his pride at first, but it will repay him in increased sexual pleasure. The reason for this is that if a man's wife gets more out of sex, he himself is going to benefit the most.

To increase your sexual responsiveness, let your wife take the top position when she wishes. Your willingness to do so will excite her and make her happy. Try letting her set the pace of lovemaking; see if she wants to choose the time and make the pass. She can teach you better ways of exciting her, and the two of you can learn new and more effective lovemaking techniques. The end result is better sex for both of you.

#7. Discover the Joy of Slow, Sensual Lovemaking.

Steps Two and Three of the Sensual Union outline ways of exploring the wife's body to find new and delightful ways of exciting her. One key feature of these techniques is for the husband and wife to move through the excitement phase of intercourse together. Usually, this means that the man gets to discover—and appreciate—the joy of slow, sensual lovemaking.

The natural urge may be to begin vaginal intercourse as quickly as possible, but the longer you can postpone this, the more you'll add to your sexual pleasure. By waiting until your wife is fully aroused, you'll guarantee that the intercourse will be mutually satisfying. Your wife will be more passionate, and so will you. The ways to go more slowly with lovemaking are:

    ● *Practice until you're an expert at performing the techniques described in Steps Two and Three of the Sensual Union.* Explore your mate's body, and learn the slow, delightful ways of arousing her. Then swap places so that she can enjoy stimulating you.

    ● *Use Step Five of the Sensual Union to bring your wife's excitement to the boiling point.* Bring her to the point of orgasm by giving her mouth-genital or clitoral stimulation. See if you can hold off inserting the penis until she begs for it!

    ● *Once you've begun intercourse, put off your climax as long as possible.* By controlling your thoughts, you can put off the pitch of excitement that would soon lead to orgasm. You may have to stop your thrusting motions for a time (or she may have to stop hers, if she's on top). Just holding the penis in the vagina is enjoyable, and it will let your excitement simmer down. After a few moments you'll be able to continue intercourse without fear of an immediate orgasm. Your wife will appreciate your slow passion, and when you do have your climax it will be that much more enjoyable for both of you.

#8. Use Your "Second" Sex Organ to Elicit Passion.

    Your tongue is your "second" sex organ. Learn to use it to show your love and to give your wife pleasure. The mouth-genital techniques outlined in Steps Five and Six of the Sensual Union are not the only ways you can use your tongue. A wife enjoys stimulation of her ears, eyes, nipples and other body parts by her husband's tongue. The tongue makes words, and these, too, can excite your wife.

How Scott Added to His Wife's Pleasure in a Special Way

    Scott was a successful salesman and a happily married father of three. Though they were in their late forties, he and his wife Mary enjoyed sex more than they had twenty years earlier. "It's because he's so sexy," Mary said with a smile.

"She's the passionate one," Scott maintained. "All I do is get her started."

One of his techniques was to whisper in Mary's ear. Before intercourse he'd promise her what he was going to do, and he'd keep his promises during their lovemaking. The whispers added to his wife's passion. Scott also found that by saying "That's too good!" or "I can't take any more of that!" he could hasten his wife's orgasm when he was about to have his own climax.

A sexually responsive husband can think of dozens of things to whisper to his wife at the right moment. He should say what he feels and what he's thinking. "I love you" and "I want you" are good to start. From there, use your own expressions. Your wife may surprise you by whispering the same words that have been on your mind!

#9. Share Your Sexual Turn-Ons with Your Wife.

Men have sexual fantasies, but so do women. There's no harm in telling your wife about these, because she's the one who can fulfill your dreams! Let her know what stimulates you, and ask her what special things turn her on. It may be that both of you are turned on by the same things.

The Joyful Thing
Fred Learned about His Wife

Fred, like many men, enjoyed viewing the sexy pictures in certain male-oriented magazines such as *Playboy*. For several years Fred was too shy to admit this to his wife, Mary Jane, though she would sometimes find copies of such magazines hidden in his chest of drawers. Then one night she caught him looking through an issue. Fred started to apologize, but his wife wouldn't hear of it.

"I've looked through those," she said, "and some of the pictures turn me on. What I like even more is when they show a man's body. Two can play the game, you know." She produced a copy of a female-oriented magazine and flipped it open to show some sexy pictures of male models. "You see, I get just as much fun from seeing a man's body as you do from seeing a woman's."

This surprised Fred, who had presumed that all women, his wife included, were naturally modest and didn't want to see a man in the nude. Mary Jane proved that she did want to see Fred that way by asking him to undress in front of her. He did, and they proceeded to have the most enjoyable sex of their marriage.

#10. Discover the Secret of Sexual Attractiveness.

The secret of a husband's sexual attractiveness is for him to love his wife. It's that simple! Love does conquer all. Be sweet to your wife. Do things for her. Consider her feelings in everything you do, and give her a part in the decision making. Be gentle in your lovemaking, and put her wishes first. Your love will make you attractive to her, and you'll have a perfect Sensual Union because of it.

13

Birth Control Methods for the Wife

A woman has more birth control methods to choose from than does a man, because by tradition she has taken the responsibility for birth control. This is changing. Husband and wife must share this responsibility, and doing so is an important part of the Sensual Union. This chapter takes up the birth control methods for the wife, and those for the husband are discussed in the following chapter.

Birth Control Methods for the Wife	
Method	*Success Rate*
Rhythm	70-85%
Vaginal foams and jellies	75-85%
Diaphragm and jelly	90-95%+
Intrauterine device (IUD)	92-98%
The Pill	99%+
Tubal Ligation	100%

Deciding on the Method That Is Right for You

The methods of birth control that are available to a woman include:

1. The rhythm method.
2. Vaginal foams and jellies.
3. Diaphragm and jelly.
4. The intrauterine device (IUD).
5. The Pill.
6. Tubal ligation.

Many things may affect your choice of a birth control method. Among these are your age, general health, frequency of intercourse, and whether you've had children. The Pill isn't safe for women with certain health problems, and it tends to cause serious side effects when a woman beyond the age of thirty-five or forty takes it. The intrauterine device works better in a woman who has had at least one child, but even so, it may cause side effects such as spotting between periods. The diaphragm in combination with vaginal jelly, especially when the husband wears a condom, is an excellent means of birth control. However, unlike the Pill and the IUD, the diaphragm must be used before each act of intercourse. Thus, it's more suited to the couple who have relations two or three times a week than to the husband and wife who make love much more often. The rhythm method offers less protection than the above methods, but it is a useful form of birth control for many couples.

To make an intelligent choice of birth control, you need to know how pregnancy happens and how the various birth control methods work to prevent it.

How Pregnancy Happens

Sexual intercourse creates pregnancy, of course, but only when the husband's sperm fertilizes his wife's egg. The man's sperm cells (hundreds of millions of them) are contained in his semen and are released at ejaculation. They enter the womb and make their way to the tubes, then swim outward in search of an egg to fertilize. Fertilization is the uniting of a sperm and egg to create what will grow into a baby. This joining of sperm and egg, which is known as *conception*, can only occur when sperm are able to reach the woman's tubes, and when an egg is waiting there for them.

A woman releases an egg from one of her ovaries each month. This event, known as *ovulation*, occurs midway between periods of bleeding. Upon its release, the egg is swept into the tube and begins a slow descent toward the womb. For a pregnancy to occur, the egg must be fertilized by a sperm within twenty-four hours. If it isn't, the egg will die. Sperm cells can live for only two or three days in the tubes, and after this length of time, they also die. Thus, pregnancy can occur if the couple have intercourse anytime between two or three days before the wife ovulates or within about twenty-four hours after she releases her egg.

How Birth Control Works

Birth control works by interfering with one of the steps leading up to pregnancy. The method may keep the woman from releasing an egg (the Pill), prevent the fertilized egg from implanting in the womb (the IUD), kill sperm cells (vaginal foam), or kill sperm and block them from entering the uterus (diaphragm and jelly). The rhythm method works in a different way. The husband and wife avoid having intercourse during days of the month when a pregnancy is most likely to occur.

The Rhythm Method

The rhythm method, also known as "the safe period," is the least expensive means of birth control and one that is acceptable to people of all religions. Three things are necessary for "rhythm" to work: (1) The wife's menstrual periods must occur at regular intervals, (2) She must know when she ovulates, and (3) She and her husband must avoid having intercourse for three days before and three days after this date.

(1) The woman's periods must occur regularly, because that is the only way that her time of ovulation can be predicted. The periods are least likely to be regular in women in their early and mid teens, and in women over the age of forty. Menstruation is most likely to be regular and predictable when the wife is between the ages of eighteen and thirty-five.

(2) Predicting the date of ovulation in a woman whose periods are regular is not too difficult. About one out of four women can tell that ovulation has occurred because the release of an egg causes her to have pain in the lower abdomen on the right or left side. The pain may last for several hours, and is fairly regular in its occurrence from one month to the next. Slight bleeding from the ovary that released the egg causes this pain. Another sign of ovulation is that a woman's sexual desire may increase sharply at this time of the month. The best way to tell when ovulation occurs, however, is to keep a temperature chart for three or four months in a row. Naturally it is necessary to use some other method of birth control during this time—some method other than the Pill, which prevents ovulation.

Take your oral temperature each morning before you get out of bed; record the reading on the calendar. Begin the chart on the first day of menstrual bleeding (called Day One), and continue it until the first day of the following period. Then, the chart starts over for the next month. You'll find that your temperature will go up about half a degree Farenheit midway through the cycle, and that the morning readings will remain elevated until the onset of bleeding. *The day your temperature rises is the day your ovary released an egg. In most women, ovulation occurs about fourteen days before the beginning of the next menstrual bleeding.* Don't worry if you don't note a change in temperature during the first month of charting. Occasionally, a normal woman won't release an egg during her cycle and no temperature change will occur. Just continue keeping the chart until you do notice the temperature change and are able to predict the day in your cycle that you will ovulate.

(3) Having intercourse only during safe times is possible when you can look ahead to the next month and know the date that you

will ovulate. Count the number of days from the onset of your menstrual bleeding (Day One) until you ovulated as determined by the temperature charts you kept. If the number of days differed slightly, take an average. Then, calculate your predicted date of ovulation for the coming month. Mark an ''X'' through this day on the calendar, and cross out the three days before and after it. Let's say, for example, that the interval between the first day of bleeding for one period and the first day of bleeding for the following period was 28 days. Your temperature rose on Day 14, indicating your release of an egg on this date. Therefore, for the upcoming month you'd avoid having intercourse on Day 14 (whatever day of the month that happened to fall on), as well as three days before it (Days 11, 12 and 13) and three days after it (Days 15, 16 and 17). For this one week during your cycle, intercourse isn't safe. Even during unsafe days, however, you can still enjoy sex. Your husband can bring you to climax with clitoral or mouth-genital stimulation, or you can bring him to orgasm by sucking his penis or stimulating it with your hand. Or, the two of you can have intercourse that is protected by another birth control method, such as the husband wearing a condom while his wife uses vaginal foam or a diaphragm and jelly.

How the Rhythm Method Worked for Becky

Becky M. and her husband, Rush, had been married two years and had two small children. For religious reasons, the rhythm method was the only one they could use. Becky kept a chart of her morning temperatures, and discovered that she ovulated on Day 15 of a 30-day cycle. By avoiding intercourse from Days 12 to 18 of each cycle, Becky and Rush were able to go three years without a pregnancy. Then Becky got pregnant, but she said it was because she and her husband had decided to have another child and had stopped using the rhythm method.

Between 15 and 30% of women who rely on the rhythm method for birth control will get pregnant during a year's time. In other words, rhythm isn't the best way to avoid pregnancy. However, even if you don't choose to use rhythm as your main way to prevent conception, you should be aware of how it works. It can be useful to know that intercourse for a week or so after your period and for a week or so just before the onset of the next period is safe.

Vaginal Foams and Jellies

Vaginal foams and jellies contain a chemical that kills sperm cells on contact (it's called a *spermicidal agent*). The woman puts the contraceptive material into her vagina before having intercourse, and it protects her by killing the husband's sperm cells. These products can be bought without a prescription, and some of the reliable brand names are Delfen, Emko, and Ramses. Follow the accompanying instructions carefully, and remember that a foaming agent tends to be more effective than jelly or cream. This is because the foam, which looks like shaving cream, spreads evenly throughout the vagina. It must be inserted with an applicator, and an applicator is also needed to instill jelly or cream into the vagina. However, foam tablets can be inserted with the fingers. Some precautions about foams and jellies are:

1. *Intercourse can begin immediately after the foam is put into the vagina*, and shouldn't be delayed for more than fifteen minutes. After this time, the foam may lose its effectiveness.
2. *Intercourse must be delayed for ten or fifteen minutes* after insertion of a foam tablet, to allow the product to dissolve. Sometimes it doesn't dissolve very well, which is why the tablet is less effective than foam, jelly or cream. A few minutes delay is also advisable after use of a cream or jelly, to give the product time to spread throughout the vagina.
3. *The foam should be left in the vagina for eight hours after having intercourse.* Douching must be postponed until after this interval of time.

4. *Another application of foam, jelly or cream* is necessary before each act of intercourse.

Some couples consider the foam or jelly too messy for frequent use. (Jelly tends to be messier than foam or cream.) The woman may object to the douching she feels is necessary to remove the spermicidal agent. The product may furnish too much lubrication for enjoyable intercourse, or it may irritate the penis. Another disadvantage is the need to keep the product handy, not always easy when intercourse occurs in some place other than the home. Perhaps the biggest drawback to using foam or jelly is its failure rate. The yearly pregnancy rate is 15 to 25% for couples who rely on this method, and this is unacceptably high. An excellent way to increase the effectiveness of foam is for the husband to wear a condom. Foam is also useful as an extra precaution for the woman with an IUD. The bottom line about foam is that it is more trouble and less effective than a well-fitting diaphragm.

Diaphragm and Jelly

The diaphragm is a dome-shaped cap of latex rubber that the wife can insert to cover the mouth of her womb (cervix). Spermicidal jelly goes in the cup of the diaphragm so that once the unit is in place the jelly will surround the cervix and be in contact with it. The diaphragm serves as a barrier to sperm, and the jelly will kill the sperm cells that do manage to wiggle around it and approach the mouth of the womb.

Who Can Use a Diaphragm

The diaphragm can be used by a bride or by a woman who has been married for over twenty years. It's a good idea, however, for the wife to wait until several weeks after marriage before obtaining one. The onset of regular sexual relations may cause her vagina to enlarge, and a diaphragm that is fitted before marriage may soon be too small to do its job properly. After the birth of a child, a new, larger diaphragm may be needed.

Some wives object to inserting the diaphragm. Squeamishness about this maneuver tends to disappear after the first few times, and some couples enjoy making insertion of the diaphragm part of their love play. Still, the wife who objects strongly to the manipulation that is necessary to use the diaphragm probably should choose another method of birth control.

How to Obtain a Diaphragm

A doctor's prescription is required before you can purchase a diaphragm. The unit must cover the cervix and stay in place behind the pubic bone, and this means that it must be fitted to each woman. The doctor will examine you and measure you for the right size of diaphragm before he writes the prescription for it. He will (or should) show you how to insert it. You can practice putting in one of the fitting rings or the diaphragm itself while you're in the examining room; the doctor can then check your technique to make sure that you did it right.

How to Use It

The four steps to using a diaphragm are (1) Prepare it properly, (2) Insert it the right way, (3) Check its position, and (4) Leave it in for a sufficient time after intercourse.

(1) Prepare the diaphragm by wetting it with warm water and squeezing a teaspoonful of spermicidal jelly into it. Some good brand names of jelly are Ramses, Delfen and Ortho, though other brands may work as well. Spread the cream around the bottom of the cup, and make sure to put some of it along the inside rim of the diaphragm.

(2) Insert the diaphragm so that it covers the top wall of your

vagina from front to back. Insertion is easier if you squat, sit on the toilet or stand with one leg resting on the toilet seat. Squeeze the flexible metal rim together with the fingers of one hand, and with your other hand spread the lips of the vulva. Then, insert the diaphragm high into the vagina until you feel it lock into place behind your cervix. Make sure the front edge is behind the pubic bone that lies just above the entrance to the vagina.

(3) *Check the diaphragm's position one last time.* Make sure you feel the firm round tip of your womb through the soft rubber of the diaphragm. If you have it in right, the diaphragm will stay in place and yet you can't feel it.

(4) *Leave the diaphragm in for 8 hours after intercourse.* This usually means until the next morning, when it's all right to remove and clean the unit before storing it for next usage. Do not take a douche immediately after intercourse when you've used the diaphragm for birth control! The stream of water might dislodge the diaphragm and allow a pregnancy to occur. Sometimes a woman forgets and leaves the diaphragm in for a day or two. This isn't harmful. However, the unit ought to be removed and cleansed once a day. It also must be filled with a fresh supply of spermicidal jelly within six hours before having intercourse.

Benefits of the Diaphragm

The diaphragm is a very effective means of birth control. Only five or ten percent of women who use this method will get pregnant during a year's time. Careful attention to the proper use of the diaphragm can make it about 98% effective in preventing pregnancy. The most common cause of failure is neglecting to put the diaphragm in before intercourse. Protection against pregnancy is even greater when the husband does his part by wearing a condom.

The diaphragm doesn't cause side effects, and is particularly suited to the couple who have intercourse only once or twice a week. One other benefit is that it can be used by the wife to cover her cervix during her menstrual period. It will hold back the menstrual flow for half an hour so that the couple can have sexual relations if they wish.

The Intrauterine Device (IUD)

The intrauterine device, or IUD, is a small piece of flexible plastic or metal that can be inserted into the womb and left there to prevent a pregnancy. (The womb is the uterus, hence the word "intrauterine.") The IUD works by keeping the fertilized egg from implanting in the womb. This is an excellent form of birth control for some women, but others have difficulty with it.

Who Can Use It

An IUD works better after a pregnancy, because the womb is larger and better able to accommodate it. However, some women who've never been pregnant can use the IUD. A pelvic exam will show whether or not you're a candidate.

How to Get an IUD

A physician must insert the IUD. This means that he'll examine you first and then choose an intrauterine device that is suitable to the size, shape and position of your womb. The ideal time for installation is during a menstrual period. The fact that you're having your period means you aren't pregnant, and it would be too late for an IUD to help you if you were. Also, the mouth of the womb enlarges slightly during the menstrual flow, making it easier to insert the device.

Effects of an IUD

Insertion may be painful. Some women develop "cramps" or experience heavy bleeding after the IUD is in place. More often, the IUD goes in with a minimum of difficulty. Very rarely an IUD may perforate through the womb and into the stomach cavity; surgery may be necessary to remove it.

Adjusting to the IUD takes time. The first few months after its insertion are when it is most likely to fall out, or to cause side effects. It may give rise to spotting between periods, heavier menstrual periods, back pain or cramps. These symptoms tend to lessen after a few months, but they may be bad enough to warrant removal of the IUD.

Effectiveness and Advantages

The success rate of an IUD is 92-98%, which means that only 2-8% of women using this method of birth control will get pregnant during a year's time. The effectiveness tends to increase when the woman has worn the IUD for a year or more.

An advantage of the intrauterine device is that once it's in place, it's there. The wife doesn't have to consult the calendar, take a pill each day, or go through the manipulation of inserting a diaphragm. However, *the use of spermicidal foam in conjunction with the IUD is indicated during the first six months of its use*. The reason for this is that it takes about six months for the body to adjust to the device and for it to work most successfully in preventing a pregnancy. Some women prefer to use foam for extra safety around the time of ovulation no matter how long the IUD has been in place.

Three "Musts" for the IUD Wearer

Three things a woman wearing an IUD must do are: (1) Check to make sure it's still in place, (2) Notify the doctor if a pregnancy occurs, and (3) Get regular check-ups.

(1) *Check to make sure the device is in place.* This is especially important during the first three to six months after its installation, because that's when an IUD is most likely to come out. Expulsion occurs in about 10% of women fitted with an IUD. (There's a greater likelihood of the device coming out if the wearer has never been pregnant.) Each IUD is made with a tail that sticks out slightly beyond the tip of the womb so that you can check for its presence. Bear down while seated on the toilet, and feel in your vagina for the dimple-like opening of the cervix. Soft threads protruding from this opening mean that the device is in place. Absence of the threads means that the IUD has been expelled or worked its way higher into the uterus. Make your check at least every week at first, but it isn't necessary to check so often after the device has been in place for several months. Notify your physician if you discover that you can't feel the tail of the IUD. Use another means of birth control until you've been seen by the doctor. He may insert another IUD, or recommend an alternate method of birth control.

(2) *Notify the doctor if you get pregnant while an IUD is in place.* The IUD should be removed as soon as possible should you become pregnant. It's not likely that it would get into the baby's body, but it might cause you to have a miscarriage and a severe, possibly fatal infection. Removal of the device may end the pregnancy.

(3) *Get regular check-ups.* The physician will probably have you return for a check-up two or three months after he inserts the device. He'll check its position and see how you're doing. He may have you come back in six months, but after that a yearly check-up is usually sufficient. Should you decide you want to get pregnant, the physician can remove the IUD.

The Way Dorothy's IUD Worked for Her

Dorothy had two children and had taken birth-control pills to prevent another pregnancy. During an office visit, she was found to have high blood pressure. Her doctor recommended she go off the Pill to see if her blood pressure would return to normal. As an alternate method of birth control, he suggested an IUD. Dorothy agreed to try it. She did have some discomfort when it was inserted, and she noted slight vaginal bleeding several times during the next month. She returned after two months and the physician removed the IUD and replaced it with a different brand. This one did not cause spotting or pain. Dorothy wore it until she entered her menopause a few years later, and it protected her from pregnancy during these years.

The Pill

The birth control pill, or "the Pill," is so effective that only one or two out of ten-thousand women who use it will get pregnant during a year's time. It does cause side effects, however, and it isn't suitable for all women. Side effects of the Pill are tied in with the way it works to prevent pregnancy.

How the Pill Works

The Pill prevents pregnancy by lulling a woman's ovaries into believing that she is already pregnant! Each tablet contains hormones that enter the woman's circulation and take the place of her natural hormones. So long as the woman takes the Pill regularly, her ovaries remain inactive. They don't make hormones and they don't release eggs. Thus, she can't get pregnant. An advantage is that her husband needn't use a condom, nor does she have to worry with a diaphragm, foam, IUD or temperature chart. The couple can make love at any time without having to worry about pregnancy.

Side Effects

The main drawback is that in order to put the woman's ovaries to sleep, the Pill has to supply an amount of estrogen and progesterone (female sex hormones) that is greater than would be produced naturally. Increased hormone levels in the woman's body imitate some of the changes of pregnancy. Among these are:

- *Soreness in the breasts*
- *Nausea and vomiting*
- *Weight gain*
- *Headache*
- *Fatigue*

More serious side effects may occur. The woman taking birth control pills runs an increased risk of developing blood clots in her legs or other body parts, high blood pressure, diabetes and jaundice. Serious side effects are more likely to occur when the woman is above the age of thirty-five. Thus, a woman's age is an important consideration in whether she should take the Pill.

Who Can Take the Pill

The best way to tell if you're a candidate for birth-control pills is to visit your doctor for a complete check-up and a frank talk about the risks and advantages of the Pill. In general, women who have or have had the following conditions shouldn't take the Pill:

- *Blood clots in the legs or lungs.* The Pill increases the thickness of the blood and makes a recurrence of clotting more likely. Women who have bad varicose veins or who've suffered a stroke probably shouldn't take the Pill.
- *Diabetes.* The Pill tends to elevate the blood sugar and make the diabetes harder to control.
- *High blood pressure.* The Pill may raise the blood pressure and put a strain on the woman's heart and blood vessels.
- *Cancer of the breast, womb or vagina.* The sex hormone content of the Pill may cause the cancer to recur or to grow more rapidly.
- *Liver disease.* The Pill affects organs throughout the body, and it may harm the liver of someone who has liver disease. Some

women who have taken the pill for four years or longer have developed noncancerous liver tumors.

● *Migraine headaches.* The sufferer of migraine headaches may note that the Pill causes the headaches to occur more frequently.

● *Heart disease.* A heart condition may or may not keep you from taking the Pill. One serious side effect of the Pill is that for a woman beyond the age of thirty-five or forty it increases the risk of having a heart attack. For this reason, women over the age of thirty-five shouldn't take the Pill. This is particularly true if the woman smokes, because smoking increases the risk of her developing a heart or circulatory side effect of the Pill.

Which Pill Is Best?

Two types of birth-control pills are available, the combination pills and the sequential pills. Each combination pill contains both estrogen and progesterone. Sequential pills contain estrogen as the only ingredient of the pills for the first 15 days, and (in sequence) estrogen and progesterone in the pills for the last 5-6 days.

The combination pills are best. A 10 or 15 times greater pregnancy rate occurs with the sequential pills, and you're more likely to get pregnant if you miss a pill. Many different brands of combination pills are available. The lower the estrogen content of your Pill, the less your chances of developing a side effect. Combination pills with an estrogen content of 0.05 mg or less are best. Your doctor is well aware of this, and will prescribe a Pill that he feels will be safe and effective for you.

How to Use the Pill

Birth control pills imitate the function of the ovaries, so you have to take them in conjunction with the menstrual cycles. This isn't difficult. Counting the first day of menstrual bleeding as Day

One, you start the pills on Day Five. Then, take one pill at the same time each day until you've finished the month's supply. Certain brands of the Pill may be taken in a slightly different manner. Check with your physician to be sure.

Some pills are supplied for 21 days of each month, some for 28 days. With the 21-day pills, you stop for a week and have your menstrual period during this time. Pills that are supplied for 28 days do not contain a hormone during the last 7 days. You have your menstrual period at the same time you would if you were taking the pills for only 21 days, and you begin a new 28-day supply of pills as soon as you've finished the previous month's supply. Some things to remember are·

- *Your menstrual periods will probably be lighter* while taking the pills. This is a natural reaction; in fact, doctors sometimes prescribe the Pill as a cure for heavy menstrual bleeding.
- *You may spot during the middle of the month* if you miss a pill. Take it as soon as you remember it. If you spot in spite of taking the pills regularly, tell your doctor. You may need a stronger dosage of birth control pills.
- *If you forget to take one pill,* take it as soon as you can and continue with your next day's pill as usual. Most of the time this causes no problem. Forgetting two pills can (but usually doesn't) allow pregnancy to occur. Take the two pills as soon as you remember them, and use an additional method of birth control for the rest of the cycle. Forgetting to take three or more pills in a row may cause you to start your period. Check with your physician about what to do. He'll probably advise you to use an alternate method of birth control for a week, and then resume your pills as if you were starting a new cycle.
- *You can still have children after going off the Pill.* However, your natural menstrual periods may not resume immediately after you stop the Pill. Sometimes it takes several months before you're back to normal. Most doctors now agree that it's best to stop taking the Pill for several months every two years. This requires the couple to use an alternate

method of birth control, but it gives the wife's ovaries a chance to ''wake up'' and work normally for awhile.

Advantages of the Pill

Despite its side effects, the Pill is an excellent method of birth control for women under the age of thirty-five. It reduces the amount of menstrual flow, keeps the periods regular, and does away with most menstrual·cramps. It is an easy method so long as the woman remembers to take her pills. No preparatory trip to the bathroom is necessary, and the wife can relax and enjoy sex because of the high degree of protection provided by the Pill. Oral contraceptives may add to the Sensual Union in another way.

Maybe you and your husband have planned a weekend trip so that the two of you can be to yourselves for a few days. A menstrual period occurring during these few days could spoil lovemaking. However, the woman taking the Pill can delay her period by simply continuing to take the pills for a few extra days until the trip is over. (One should not make a habit of this.) Stopping the pills will allow her period to start. Seven days later she begins the next cycle of pills. The bride-to-be who begins the Pill can use it in the same way to control the onset of menstrual bleeding. Taking the Pill, she will know when her period is due and can plan her wedding date accordingly. Or, she can continue the Pill a few extra days to postpone a period that might otherwise begin on or just before the wedding date. Her doctor would be the best one to advise her on this use of the Pill.

Surgery to Prevent Pregnancy

Two types of surgery can be done to prevent a woman from becoming pregnant. One is to tie her tubes (tubal ligation), and the other is to remove her uterus (hysterectomy). The latter operation is usually reserved for the woman who has something wrong with her womb, because it is major surgery. Tubal ligation is much easier to have done.

Tubal Ligation

Each tube reaches about four inches from the ovary to the womb. The traditional way to tie the tubes is to make an incision between the pubic region and the navel while the woman is under general anesthesia. It isn't difficult to locate the tubes where they attach to the uterus. A tie is made in two places in each tube, and the portion of the tube between the ties is cut out. This not only seals off the tube but creates a gap of an inch or so between the cut ends. The egg can't get from the ovary to the womb, and the woman can't get pregnant. The success rate (pregnancy protection) of tubal ligation is virtually 100%; about one out of 10,000 women who've had the operation will get pregnant during a year's time.

A newer way of tying the tubes is by using an instrument known as a laparoscope. It is inserted into the stomach cavity through a very small incision, and the procedure can be done in a minor surgery room without the need for the woman to be admitted to the hospital.

Indications

A sterilization operation isn't usually done unless a woman has several children. One reason for caution is that the woman may change her mind after the operation and decide that she wants a larger family. She can, of course, adopt children. In a certain percentage of cases, it's possible to reverse the tubal ligation and to restore fertility. It's best not to count on this, however, and to reserve the sterilization operation for after you've had your family and believe you and your husband aren't suited for other methods of birth control. One benefit of tubal ligation is that it may increase the wife's sexual responsiveness.

Carla's Discovery of How to
Improve Her Sexual Responsiveness

Carla, a school teacher and mother of two, became pregnant with a third child when she was thirty-four. She hadn't planned on the pregnancy, and the birth occurred in the early fall so that she didn't get to teach that year. The following year she returned to work, but she told her husband, Tom, that she definitely didn't want any more children. Tom agreed and tried to reassure her that they'd be careful, but his wife seemed to lose her sex drive. It was as if she worried so much about getting pregnant, she couldn't relax and enjoy sex.

She was too old for birth control pills, and didn't trust the diaphragm. (Her third pregnancy occurred when she made the mistake of failing to insert the diaphragm on one occasion.) She tried an IUD, but developed heavy bleeding that required its removal. Finally she and her husband discussed the possibility of a sterilization operation. Tom didn't want to have a vasectomy, but he was agreeable if his wife wanted to have a tubal ligation.

Carla was surprised to learn how easy it was to have the operation. She and Tom signed the form, and the surgery was done one morning in an outpatient surgical center. Carla went home that afternoon, remained in bed a day, and was back to normal the following week. The best thing about the experience was how she felt afterward.

"It's just such a sense of relief," she said. "I didn't realize how much the fear of another pregnancy was affecting my relations with Tom. Now I'm more open and loving with him, and he's the same with me. Things have never been so good for us."

Methods That Don't Work

Three birth control methods that don't work are the douche, the woman's failure to have an orgasm, and the use of feminine hygiene preparations. Douching after intercourse is not a good birth control mehtod because it's impossible to wash all the sperm out of the vagina. Some of them enter the womb immediately after ejaculation, and the douche water will wash still others up into the cervix. A woman's failure to have an orgasm in no way keeps her from becoming pregnant. A man's sperm can still fertilize her egg. Finally, the use of Norforms and other hygienic products does not prevent pregnancy.

Coitus interruptus—the withdrawal of the man's penis before ejaculation—is another birth control method that doesn't work too well. It and other birth control methods for the husband are the subject of the next chapter.

14

Birth Control Methods for the Husband

The husband and wife share equally in producing a baby, and they should share equally in preventing pregnancy. Doing so can actually improve the quality of the Sensual Union. A woman who knows that her husband is willing to do his part in birth control will naturally be more sexually responsive than the wife who must carry this burden alone. And the husband may discover that sharing this responsibility can add to his sexual pleasure.

Birth Control Methods for the Husband	
Method	*Success Rate*
Rhythm	70-85%
Coitus interruptus	70-80%
Condom	85-95%
Condom & diaphragm	98% +
Vasectomy*	100%

*After the man's semen is shown to contain no sperm cells.

Choice of Methods for the Husband

Birth control methods for the husband are designed to keep the sperm from entering the womb and fertilizing an egg. The ways to accomplish this are:

1. The rhythm method.
2. Coitus interruptus.
3. The condom.
4. Vasectomy.

The Rhythm Method

The rhythm method was discussed in the previous chapter. It is the technique of determining the time during her menstrual cycle when the wife is most likely to become pregnant, and avoiding intercourse during these seven days. It is a method for the husband for the simple reason that he must cooperate for it to work. What happens when he doesn't cooperate can be shown by the case of

The Man Who Got Sexy at the Wrong Time

Charles W. was the husband of a young woman I shall call Suzy. I delivered Suzy's third child, and before she left the hospital she asked for an effective means of birth control. "And I mean something other than rhythm," she said with a sigh. "My husband just won't cooperate on that one." Suzy went on to describe how, because of their religion, she and Charles used rhythm after they had the two children they had planned to have. It worked for a few months, but then Charles started getting sexy at the wrong time of the month. "He knew from what I showed him on the calendar when it wasn't safe to have intercourse, but he just ignored it. He made a game out of trying to seduce me when I was most fertile, and"—she nodded toward the nursery—"he succeeded."

Because Suzy had a heart murmur, I was able to arrange for her to have a tubal ligation to prevent the damage to her health that another pregnancy might cause. But her husband's lack of cooperation is an example of why the rhythm method may fail. Three ways a man can contribute to the success of rhythm are:

1. *Understand how rhythm works.* Read the previous chapter, and help your wife to keep the temperature chart that will show the time of the month when she is most fertile.
2. *Do your part by not attempting to have intercourse during the "unsafe" days of the month.* You may stimulate your wife to orgasm during this interval by mouth-genital or direct clitoral stimulation, and she can give you pleasure by stimulating the penis with her mouth or hand. But vaginal intercourse is not safe!
3. *Use an effective means of birth control if you do have intercourse during the unsafe days.* Some couples using rhythm prefer to continue having relations during the time of a wife's peak fertility. One reason may be that the wife often experiences a greater sexual drive at this time of the month. To prevent pregnancy, the couple must use another means of birth control. A convenient method is for the wife to use spermicidal foam or a diaphragm and jelly, while the husband wears a condom.

Coitus Interruptus

Coitus interruptus, or withdrawal, is when the man removes his penis from the vagina just before he ejaculates. It is a poor method of birth control. About 20-30% of couples using this method alone will have a pregnancy during a year's time. Most persons feel that this is an unacceptably high risk. Some reasons for the ineffectiveness of this method are:

1. *The husband is the one who is responsible for withdrawing the penis before ejaculation.* This requires him to know when ejaculation is about to occur, and to withdraw beforehand. However, a man has only 3 seconds of warning

between when he knows that he is going to ejaculate and when he actually does. These several seconds occur at the time when his enjoyment is at its highest. His natural urge is to drive the penis deeper into the vagina and hold it there. The rational act of withdrawal may not be possible at such an irrational moment.

2. *The husband who has had several drinks or is under the influence of any other drug shouldn't use coitus interruptus.* He probably won't be sufficiently alert to remove the penis before ejaculation.

3. *The fluid that escapes from the penis before ejaculation may contain enough sperm cells to cause pregnancy.* Thus, the wife may get pregnant even when her husband withdraws before ejaculation.

4. *Some couples make the mistake of resuming intercourse after the man has ejaculated.* This can lead to pregnancy because the man's penis is not empty. Sperm cells may remain in the penis for several hours after ejaculation, and can enter the wife's birth tract to cause a pregnancy.

Even if he learns to withdraw his penis before ejaculation, the husband will not get as much pleasure from coitus interruptus as he would from completing intercourse the natural way. His wife may also feel frustrated. Her sexual excitement tends to rise more slowly than her husband's, and she may need and want more stimulation just at the moment when he must break off his lovemaking. In fact, she may give in to her own natural urges and prevent the withdrawal of the penis. The most favorable thing about coitus interruptus is that it is safer than ejaculating into the vagina. The husband and wife who are serious about birth control should choose another method.

The Condom

The condom ("rubber" or "prophylactic") is a sheath the husband wears over his penis during intercourse. It is a tried and proven method of birth control, and offers a success rate of between 85-95% among couples who rely on this method alone. In fact, the degree of protection offered by a condom can be uniformly high when it is used properly and when the wife uses a method of her own such as the diaphragm and jelly.

Things You Should Know about the Condom

The condom is said to be the most commonly used birth control method in the world. For many years, however, it had a bad reputation in the United States. One bought rubbers from a dispenser in the rest room of a gas station, or from a druggist who might have been as embarrassed to produce them from beneath the counter as you were to ask. The condom came to be associated with illicit sex, venereal disease and vulgarity. It was apt to break during intercourse, and by its very design it tended to detract from the enjoyment of sex. All this has changed. The manufacture and sale of condoms is now regulated by the Food and Drug Administration, and the quality of the product has improved greatly. Over forty states now have laws permitting druggists to display condoms above the counter. This enables the purchaser to select the item he wants much as he might select a preferred brand of aspirin or laxative. The result has been a great upsurge in the popularity of the condom.

One reason for its acceptability is that the condom causes no side effects. The husband who uses it can take charge of birth control. He can save his wife from having to worry about the possibility of developing a blood clot or heart disease from the Pill, and spare her the cramps or spotting between periods she might get from an IUD. The Pill must be taken every day, and an IUD must be worn continuously. The condom is necessary only during intercourse. What's more, it's small and can be carried anywhere. Better manufacturing has meant more effective condoms and also more sensitive ones.

The Variety of Condoms

The two main types of condoms are those made from latex rubber (hence the name, "rubbers") and those made from animal membranes. The two differ in price, sensitivity and in the way they are stored and used.

● *Latex condoms* are less expensive than those made from animal membranes. They're also less sensitive. This is not to say that the latex condom is inferior, for it isn't. It does its job quite well, and can be bought unlubricated or prelubricated with a moist substance or with a powdery, silicone-type lubricant. Latex condoms are available in exotic, decorative colors, and some brands are textured to provide the wife more stimulation. Still others have reservoir tips or "ticklers" on the end.

● *Membrane condoms*, or "skins," are made from the intestinal membranes of sheep. Most are imported from Australia and New Zealand. These condoms are more expensive than latex condoms, but many users believe the extra price is worth paying. The membrane condom conducts heat much better than does latex rubber, and intercourse has a more natural feeling. In fact, a man wearing a good quality skin is scarcely aware of it during intercourse. All membrane condoms are lubricated, and each must be kept tightly sealed in its package until just before use. A disadvantage of the skin condom is that it is more likely to slip off during intercourse than is a latex condom. Lubricated condoms of either type may slip off the penis, but the lubrication also has its advantages.

The Couple Who Discovered an Easy Way to the Sensual Union

Mr. and Mrs. M., a couple in their early fifties, still enjoyed having sexual relations at least once a week. However, Mrs. M.'s menopause had caused her to develop some dryness of the vagina. Even at the peak of her sexual excitement she didn't produce enough vaginal lubrication. She considered asking her doctor for an estrogen-containing vaginal cream, but her husband had a better idea. He purchased a supply of membrane condoms. "We didn't need them for birth control," he told me, "but they did solve this other problem." The membrane condoms, which were moist and slick, provided just the right amount of lubricant to make inter-course enjoyable. Mr. and Mrs. M. also reported that the membrane condoms did not detract from the pleasure of sexual relations.

How to Use the Condom

Couples who take the time to use the condom correctly will find that it is a safe and easy means of birth control. Here are six ways to make sure that the condom does its job:

(1) Purchase good-quality condoms. Condoms can be stored for about two years, but those sold in dispensing machines may be older than this. The problem is, you don't know how long they've been in the machine. The best idea is to buy condoms from a drugstore. If you don't wish to purchase them in a store where you're a regular customer, pick some up next time you're in a nearby city. One man I know does not like to buy condoms and be checked out by the young woman at the cash register. His wife knows the right brand, and she buys them! As an alternative, you can purchase condoms by mail from any of the reputable companies that provide this service.

(2) Put the condom on at the start of sex play. Do not get into the habit of having intercourse without the condom right up until the point of ejaculation, and then putting the condom on. For one thing, the penis will be slippery and the condom may not stay on. Also, semen may escape from the penis before ejaculation, and the sperm cells in it can cause pregnancy! Finally, the man who waits runs the same risk as the man who depends on coitus interruptus. He may not withdraw in time. Putting the condom on at the start of sex play makes for smoother, uninterrupted lovemaking.

The Couple Who Made a Game
Out of Birth Control

Mary Beth and Jack C. had tried many methods of birth con-trol, and had decided that for them, the condom in conjunction with the diaphragm and jelly was best. They made a game of inserting the diaphragm and applying the condom. They'd begin their foreplay in various ways, and gradually build excitement through the techniques described in the Sensual Union. At some point before intercourse, however, Jack would insert his wife's diaphragm—or watch her insert it. She, in turn, would apply the condom to his penis—or watch him apply it. They found this to be a sensuous and pleasant part of foreplay, and their method of birth control was completely effective.

(3) Use a premoistened condom unless the wife has an abundance of natural oils. Latex rubber can irritate the vagina if the wife's natural lubricant is insufficient to protect her. Saliva can help to moisten a dry condom. Or, body oil or spermicidal jelly can be used as a lubricant. Vaseline should not be used; it destroys latex rubber. In general, it's better to buy a premoistened condom than to apply lubricant to an unmoistened one.

(4) Check to make sure the condom is in place after intercourse begins. A husband's hands are busy stimulating his wife's body during intercourse, but he can easily take the time to make sure that his condom is still in place. It's especially important to check the position of a membrane condom, which has a greater tendency to slide off. The ideal position is for the condom to cover the entire penis and the rubber ring to fit snugly around the base of the organ. A very important point is to keep some slack at the end of the condom. This makes room for the semen that will be deposited there at the time of ejaculation. The wife may enjoy learning to assist her husband in applying the condom and in making sure that it remains in place.

(5) Remove the penis from the vagina a minute or two after ejaculation. Continued thrusting may cause the condom to slip off. Removal of the penis shortly after ejaculation will prevent the loss of semen into the vagina. Be sure to hold the rubber ring of the condom in place around the hilt of the penis during withdrawal.

(6) Use a new condom for each act of intercourse. Reuse of a condom is not a good idea. Use a new one every time you make love.

The Condom in Conjunction with Other Methods

Used correctly, the condom by itself is a good method of birth control. When the wife uses diaphragm and jelly and the husband wears a condom, the degree of protection is 98% or better—an effectiveness approaching that of the Pill! The combination of condom and diaphragm is especially useful when the wife is between the age of 35 and menopause. The condom can serve as a supplement to other methods of birth control:

● *Couples practicing the rhythm method* may want to have intercourse during the unsafe days. The man can wear a condom, and the wife should use foam or a diaphragm and jelly.

● *The wife who uses foam as her main method of birth control* will get much more protection against pregnancy when her husband does his part by wearing a condom.

● *The woman who wears an IUD* can have almost 100% protection against pregnancy if she uses foam and her husband uses a condom during the seven most fertile days of her menstrual cycle. Additional protection in the middle of the woman's cycle is needed during the first six months after the IUD is put into the uterus. However, the wisest course is to continue the foam and condom during fertile days even after the IUD has been in place for six months.

● *The wife who forgets to take the Pill* for two or three days may become pregnant if she has intercourse at this time. Her husband can help to protect her by using a condom until she's back to regular on the Pill.

Vasectomy

Vasectomy is the sterilization operation for a man. Each of the two tubes carrying sperm from the testicles to the penis is a *vas deferens*, thus the name, *vasectomy*. The operation is easy to perform. The doctor injects local anesthetic, makes a small cut, locates each vas deferens, and places two ties around it. He cuts out the portion in between the ties. (Other techniques, just as effective, are in common use.) The procedure can be done in the office, and the man can walk out afterwards. He has to avoid having intercourse for several days, but when he does return to sexual relations he'll notice no decrease in the amount of his semen. The reason for this is that the sperm accounts for only 5% of the volume of the semen. Most of the semen comes from the prostate and seminal vesicles, and a vasectomy does not interfere with the release of these secretions. One thing the man must realize, however, is that he doesn't become sterile until some time after the vasectomy.

The reason for this is that sperm cells can live for several weeks in the part of the vas deferens above the cut (that is, between the point of the vasectomy and the place where the sperm ducts enter the penis). As a rule, twelve ejaculations are necessary to remove all the sperm from the uppermost parts of the sperm ducts. A physician must examine the semen and certify that it is free of sperm cells before the man can be sure that he is sterile.

A drawback to vasectomy is that the man may object to having to perform masturbation to give samples of his semen for examination. Or, the husband may harbor the conviction that the operation will deprive him of his manhood or sex drive. It won't. The cells that make his sex hormone are unaffected by the operation. In fact, he may have a greater sex drive because he no longer has to worry about causing a pregnancy.

What if the man changes his mind and decides to have another child? Vasectomy can be reversed in most instances by the use of a microsurgical technique. However, the operation is not always successful in restoring fertility, especially when the man had the vasectomy ten years or more previously. The reason is that during the time the sperm ducts are tied off, the man may develop a natural resistance to his own sperm cells. The best course, then, is for the couple to make sure they want no more children before the husband has a vasectomy.

Bibliography

Abse, D. Wilfred, Ethel M. Nash, and Lois M. R. Louden, *Marital & Sexual Counseling in Medical Practice*, 2nd Edition, Harper & Row, New York, 1974.

Allen, Gina and Clement G. Martin, *Intimacy, Sensitivity, Sex, and the Art of Love*, Cowles Book Company, Inc., Chicago, 1971.

Brooks, M. H., "Effect of Diabetes on Female Sexual Response," *Medical Aspects of Human Sexuality*, February, 1977, pp. 63-64.

Deaton, John, *A Medical Doctor's Guide to Youth, Health, and Longevity*, Parker Publishing Company, Inc., West Nyack, New York, 1977.

Deaton, John G., *Below the Belt: A Book about the Pelvic Organs*, Franklin Publishing Company, Palisade, New Jersey, 1978.

Deutsch, Ronald M., *The Key to Feminine Response in Marriage*, Random House, New York, 1968.

Dudley, D. L., "Sexual Activity for Asthmatics—a Psychiatric Perspective," *Medical Aspects of Human Sexuality*, November, 1976, pp. 63-64.

Eichenlaub, John E., *The Marriage Art*, Lyle Stuart, New York, 1961.

Ellis, Albert, *The Art and Science of Love*, Lyle Stuart, New York, 1960.

Finnerty, Frank A., Jr. and Shirley Motter Linde, *High Blood Pressure*, David McKay Company, New York, 1975.

Fleming, Alice, *Nine Months, An Intelligent Woman's Guide to Pregnancy,* Stein and Day, New York, 1972.

Glover, Benjamin H., "Sex Counseling of the Elderly," *Hospital Practice,* June, 1977, pp. 101-113.

Hall, R. E., *Sex, An Advanced Primer,* Doubleday, New York, 1974.

Hellman, Louis M. and Jack A. Pritchard, *Williams Obstetrics,* 14th Edition, Appleton-Century-Crofts, New York, 1971.

Hennekens, Charles H. and Brian MacMahon, "Oral Contraceptives and Myocardial Infarction," *The New England Journal of Medicine,* May 19, 1977 (vol. 296), pp. 1166-1167.

Hite, Shere, *The Hite Report,* Macmillan Publishing Company, New York, 1976.

"J," *The Sensuous Woman,* Lyle Stuart, New York, 1969.

Jacobs, L. I., "Impaired Sexual Response," *Consultant,* September, 1976, pp. 35-40.

Johnson, S.A.M., "Sexual Problems Associated with Dermatologic Conditions," *Medical Aspects of Human Sexuality,* September, 1976, pp. 157-158.

Kavanagh, Terence, *Heart Attack? Counterattack!,* Van Nostrand Reinhold, New York, 1976.

Kinsey, Alfred C., Wardell B. Pomeroy, and Clyde E. Martin, *Sexual Behavior in the Human Male,* W. B. Saunders, Philadelphia, 1948.

Kinsey, Alfred C., Wardell B. Pomeroy, Clyde E. Martin, and Paul H. Gebhard, *Sexual Behavior in the Human Female,* W. B. Saunders, Philadelphia, 1953.

Kordel, Lelord, *How to Keep Your Youthful Vitality After Forty,* G. P. Putnam's Sons, 1969, pp. 120-138.

Lamb, Lawrence E., *Your Heart and How to Live With It,* The Viking Press, New York, 1969, pp. 214-218.

Langmyhr, G. J., "Varieties of Coital Positions: Advantages and Disadvantages," *Medical Aspects of Human Sexuality,* June, 1976, pp. 128-129.

Levine, S. B., "Marital Sexual Dysfunction: Introductory Concepts," *Annals of Internal Medicine,* vol. 84, April, 1976, pp. 448-453.

Lloyd, C. W. (editor), *Human Reproduction and Sexual Behavior,* Lea & Febiger, Philadelphia, 1964.

Massie, E., "What Conditions Require a Patient to Abstain from Sexual Activity?", *Medical Aspects of Human Sexuality,* 1976, pp. 55-70.

Masters, William H. and Virginia E. Johnson, *Human Sexual Response*, Little, Brown and Co., Boston, 1966.

———, *Human Sexual Inadequacy*, Little, Brown and Co., Boston, 1970.

———, (with Robert J. Levin), *The Pleasure Bond*, Little, Brown and Co., Boston, 1970.

McCary, James L., *Human Sexuality*, Von Nostrand Reinhold, New York, 1967.

———, *Freedom and Growth in Marriage*, Hamilton Publishing Company, Santa Barbara, California, 1975.

Morgan, Marabel, *The Total Woman*, Fleming H. Revell, Old Tappan, New Jersey, 1973.

Murad, Ferid, "What You Should Know Before Prescribing an Oral Contraceptive," *Consultant*, March, 1975, pp. 187-188.

Powell, L. C., Jr., "Faster Help in Sexual Problems," *Consultant*, January, 1976, pp. 64-72.

———, "The Most Potent Aphrodisiac," *Consultant*. January, 1977, p. 58.

Renshaw, D. C., "Sexual Problems in Stroke Patients," *Medical Aspects of Human Sexuality*, December, 1975, pp. 68-74.

Reuben, David, *Any Woman Can!*, David McKay, New York, 1971.

Schoenberg, Jane and Jo Ann Stickman, *How to Survive Your Husband's Heart Attack*, David McKay Co., New York, 1974.

Smith, Donald R., *General Urology*, Lange Medical Publications, 8th Edition, Los Altos, California, 1975.

Tagatz, George E. and Richard B. McHugh, "Oral Contraceptives—a Continuing Reappraisal," *Postgraduate Medicine*, August, 1971, pp. 127-128.

Taylor, Robert B., *Feeling Alive After 65*, Arlington House Publishers, New Rochelle, New York, 1973.

The Boston Women's Health Book Collective, *Our Bodies, Ourselves*, Simon and Schuster, New York, 1971.

Tyrer, Louise B. and William A. Granzig, "Contraceptives for the teenager: things to know before prescribing," *Consultant*, November, 1975, pp. 170-179.

Weisberg, Martin, "Sexual Medicine; Female Sexuality," *The New Physician*, February, 1977, pp. 43-44.

Index